I0530721

How God Thinks

Revealing God's Heart Through the Language

of Symbolism

David Vancelette

ISBN: 978-1-963917-57-4 (Paperback)
ISBN: 978-1-963917-58-1 (Hardback)
ISBN: 978-1-963917-59-8 (Ebook)
Library of Congress Control Number: 2024920625

Printed in the United States of America.

CONTENTS

PREFACE

G od promises that times can get tough for those who want to follow Jesus. I've had my share of tough times. God had a lot to straighten out in my life, and I didn't always learn the lessons quickly. I rarely changed my ways because the Bible told me to, especially when the right way was painful or kept me from my idea of happiness. I needed to know why his way was right and mine was wrong. Still, I kept seeking God's face and he was always faithful in helping me understand.

Later in life, I began to feel that I should write some of the things I've learned. Maybe it would save somebody from making the mistakes I've made. I felt inadequate, but a quote I remembered from the University of Penn bookstore in Philadelphia forced me to press on. The quote was from Eleanor Roosevelt. She said, "You must do the thing you think you cannot do."

I soon started to write.

There were some, of course, who tried to dissuade me from writing the book, especially those who knew my past. But there were also key people who encouraged me all the way to completion. God himself, was one. He has been my constant source of strength. My editor, Bradley Harris, has been a clear spring of knowledge, good advice, and a great sense of humor. He has been invaluable to the effort. Finally, there was John Hill. He was the very first person to suggest I put my thoughts into a book over twenty-five years ago. We worked together for a number of years, and he would often end our conversations with the remark, "Write the book!"

Ultimately, all my thanks and praise go to God, who has always been a Father to the fatherless, who always watched over me and forgave me when I turned away from him. My hope is that many will come to know that God has very good reasons for demanding things we barely understand, and he feels very strongly about them. Finally, I hope the love and righteousness of every reader will shine like the sun, "so that you may become blameless and pure, children of God without fault in a crooked and depraved generation, in which you shine like stars in the universe" (Philippians 2:15).

Throughout the book, I chose to use the NIV, 1984 edition, for all my quotes (except where noted) because it's the version I've enjoyed the most and used for my Bible readings through the years. I praise God for it.

INTRODUCTION

"My people are destroyed from lack of knowledge," says Hosea 4:6. Any casual reader of Scripture can see that symbolism plays a large part of Bible interpretation from Genesis to Revelation. Some symbols are surprising and difficult to figure out. How about the woman in a bushel basket with a lead cover who represents wickedness and is carried on the wings of two other women to the land of Babylon?[1] (Surely not a favorite of the feminist movement—understandably so). Then there was the time Jesus himself drove his kosher listeners crazy when he told them to eat his body and drink his blood.[2] This was God in the flesh talking to a crowd of disciples, but it didn't seem to matter. Many stopped following him anyway even though he told them it was the *Spirit* that gives life—the flesh didn't count for anything. People have a hard time with symbolism. Since God uses it throughout Scripture, we need to pay close attention to symbolism, or we might find ourselves among those who walk away.

Today we find ourselves in a heap of trouble in the West. Long gone are the days when the typical person on the street still believes in God and that he's all-powerful, or that Jesus was God in the flesh and that he cares for and generally directs our lives. Never mind whether we should fear him or not or stop doing things that might offend him. The idea that we should have a *romantic* relationship with God sounds perfectly ridiculous to the educated elite, coming at the Bible with a morality based solely on the goodness of mankind (i.e., humanism). Christians have just about given up trying to explain the importance of marriage and the symbolism behind it. As

---

[1] Zechariah 5:5ff.
[2] John 6:53.

a result, when a group sets out to change centuries-old definitions of morality, not even Christians are prepared enough to stand against them. We have reached the point where we need to listen once again to God's heart about the things that matter so much to him, then resolve to stand by his truths no matter what the cost.

This book is not intended to be an exhaustive treatise on the metaphysics of God's mind and the spiritual mechanics involved in God's thought processes. The answers to those questions will never be known by any finite mind. My desire is that these pages will give us a better understanding of what God has revealed to us about how he thinks, especially with regard to, perhaps, his most important vehicle of communication: *symbolism*. If we understand symbolism, it will help us understand not only how he thinks, but also how he feels. Understanding God's spiritual feelings will bring an entirely new dimension to our relationship with him. This will help us overcome sin in our lives when we realize how much breaking symbolism also breaks God's heart. Understanding symbolism will also help us guide others through the difficult areas of Scripture which God's enemy has used to confuse our culture.

May the Lord help us all to understand, in some small way, how he thinks that we may be that shining light to a lost generation, for his glory.

When evening comes, you say, "It will be fair weather, for the sky is red," and in the morning, "Today it will be stormy, for the sky is red and overcast." You know how to interpret the appearance of the sky but you cannot interpret the signs of the times.

—Jesus the Messiah, Matthew 16:2

1

Symbolism

My father handed me a knife. He wanted me to kill myself.

I've heard that fathers are supposed to be the first symbol to their children of what God is like—strong and kind. At eight years old, my idea of God was not a good one. But I still loved my Dad. He earned the Silver Star, Bronze Star, and the Purple Heart in World War II. On a cold January day in 1945, near the French-German border, a platoon of men from Charlie Company, led by my father, was pinned down at the bottom of a snowy hill by two enemy machine guns. The guns were in a bunker fortified with heavy logs. The enemy gunners were firing down on them from a hundred yards away. The platoon could only return fire with handguns and rifle-grenades, not enough to take out a protected machine gun nest. My father called for a bazooka and began snaking his way up the hill with several rounds of ammunition, in full view of and under heavy fire from the machine guns. He reached a flanking position that gave him some protection from the bunker and loaded the bazooka. His first shot was a direct hit, knocking out the logs that guarded the machine guns. He reloaded, took aim, and fired again. Another direct hit. This time, two enemy soldiers were killed, and five remaining soldiers came out unarmed and surrendered to my father. This action allowed his platoon to help liberate the town of Wingen, France, on January 6, 1945. For this, he earned the Silver Star.[3] This was a man unafraid of death.

---

[3]   Galloway, Honor Roll: 276th Infantry Regiment

Despite the heroic acts Dad performed in France and Germany, he came home from the war an emotional wreck, with what we now call PTSD and a host of memories of death and destruction that haunted him till the day he died. He buried his memories in alcohol, which took an awful toll on our family. One Christmas, my mom, dad, grandparents, brother, and I were in a rickety train car on the Reading Railroad, heading into Philadelphia to see Santa at a large department store. Our train passed another one coming from the other direction. The passing train was so close, the windows rattled like a machine gun. Fully dressed in suit and tie, Dad cried out, "Down!" then dove under the seat in front of him. He embarrassed my mom and her parents, who scoffed at his mock heroism. My brother and I just stared in disbelief, thinking, "Whoa. What did the war do to our Dad?"

Sometime later, before their divorce, Dad was in the kitchen, drunk and harassing my Mom. She warned him, "Stop it. You're drunk!" I was in the next room, so I couldn't see what he was doing. I peeked around the corner and saw him standing about two paces away, trying to lift up Mom's dress.

I ran up to my dad and yelled, "Stop it or I'm gonna kill myself!" He looked at me and, without saying a word, reached into the kitchen drawer and pulled out a knife. He held it out for me to take. It was just inches away. I thought about what my father was asking me to do. For a brief moment, I thought about the pain of killing myself, plunging the knife deep into my heart. But I ran away crying instead. I refused to obey my father. Dad might not have been afraid of death, but I sure was. Neither Mom nor Dad came to me that night nor any other night for the rest of my life, to explain what had happened, or to make sure I was okay. I felt worthless and abandoned—alone.

Not much good came from that haunting episode except for one thing: it set me on a journey to find out if God was real, and if so, did he think I was worth saving, or was I worthless to him too? What if I did kill myself? One thing was sure: Killing myself would have ended my chance to learn about God from a safe distance. Instead, I would have to stand right in front of him, and say to his face, "Thanks anyway, but this life you gave me wasn't worth living." Deep down, I don't think that's what I wanted to tell Almighty God on my first visit. Thankfully, I received Jesus as my Savior at age sixteen at a church youth group. God reached down and rescued me that night.

I didn't understand as a child what my father's actions looked like from God's point of view. Now, I do. This was a case of broken symbolism. My father failed miserably at representing God to his wife and children. The reasons for his failure were understandable, if not excusable. The horrors of war are a demonic entry point into one's mind. So, too, are thoughts of suicide, which I struggled with for years to come. My father and I violated a very important symbol that God placed within every person—his precious *imago Dei*, or image of God. I didn't know it at the time, but this was my first encounter with symbolism. For years, I told God that his image within me wasn't worth living for. I didn't know how much symbolism meant to God and that, without symbolism, all our lives would be meaningless. As we will see, without symbolism, we would literally know nothing about the God who loves us and who desperately wants a relationship with us—a deeply symbolic and meaningful relationship.

Symbolism: The Basics

All of us live our lives in symbols. To help understand what that means, here's a question: what do hearts on Valentine's Day, traffic lights, red skies, each word on this page, and human sexuality have in common? "Absolutely nothing whatsoever," you might reply, incorrectly. Actually, each of these things are signs or symbols. They "stand for" something other than what their mere appearance reveals.

"Even sex?" you ask. Yes, especially sex. What's more, these examples are signs on a couple of different levels. Men are reminded annually—sometimes by girlfriends, always by greeting card companies—to respect the meaning of red hearts, and constantly by police to respect the meaning of traffic lights. The meaning behind hearts and traffic lights has been devised by man. But red skies, words, and sexuality are signs of a different kind. These are symbols whose meanings have been designed by God—a rather bold assertion, but stay tuned for the evidence.

Anyone who runs a stop light may find the police asking for a little contribution to the local PD. Even if you rail against the cheapening of Valentine's Day by the greeting card industry, you still know what a red heart means when you see one. But when the symbolism behind marriage, sexual ethics, or a host of other human experiences has been violated, God warns everyone that they risk punishment in this life as well as eternal punishment in the next. This is because God himself has instituted many such symbols in the realm of human experience that function as moral guideposts, intended to help men and women find God during their journeys on Earth. God feels deeply violated when these symbols are broken and, as I learned from my experiences as a child, even human life represents the life within God himself. For someone to take his or her own life implies that the life God gave us isn't worth living—and neither is his.

To understand why God is offended by—well, by anything that offends him—we need to understand a little more about symbolism in general and why it's so important to both God and man. The reason *we* think in symbols is because *God thinks in symbols*. Understanding symbolism is a key to understanding how God thinks, at least as far as he has revealed his thinking to us in his Word, the Bible.

This book will look at two broad categories of symbols, including how God both thinks and feels about *fulfilled* symbolism in creation and in Scripture as well as how he feels about *broken* symbolism. We'll also discuss various historical and symbolic events in the Bible, a few from history, and look at the modern-day destruction of sexual symbolism. Finally, I'll advance a theory that the Father originally intended the Lord Jesus to offer himself on the altar of the temple in Jerusalem—in a more literal fulfillment of Levitical symbolism—rather than on the cross. This would have resulted in an even greater humiliation of Satan than our current understanding of his downfall. But first, a closer look at symbolism itself.

Symbols on the Human Level

Everyone knows that words can be used to take on symbolic meaning. That's how poetry and other literature gain their power to evoke emotion using their metaphorical meaning behind the surface storyline. The plot of a good piece of literature is usually developed in such a way that it taps into powerful, universal symbols of human suffering, tragedy, victory over dire circumstances, or the triumph of love in the face of impossible odds. But there's yet another level of symbolism on the human level, usually only discussed in literary and philosophical circles. These esoteric discussions often include the notion that words themselves are entirely symbolic in nature. The fact is, you can't even speak a word without using a symbol because spoken words have no intrinsic meaning of their own.

Here's what I mean: Words are really just symbols. They are collections of letters that English speakers (in our case) have agreed upon to represent other objects or ideas. Even the letters G-o-d are completely meaningless without some agreement that the word (in English, at least) describes that all-powerful being who created heaven and earth and reveals himself in the Bible. Whenever you see or hear the word *God*, that's who you think of. It's automatic, especially in Western civilization. Every creation under heaven and every idea expressed by God and given to man is described *symbolically* by language. Even facial expressions and other nonverbals convey symbolic meaning. You simply *must* communicate using symbols—you have no other choice.

Ancient Thinkers on Symbolism

The study of signs and symbols goes back ages, to ancient times. Philosophers of old as well as modern literary authorities confirm this view that our experience is completely dependent upon interpreting symbols. Plato, in the *Cratylus*, had Hermogenes say, "No name belongs to a particular thing *by nature*."[4] Later, Aristotle expressed

---

[4] Chandler, 26, quoting Plato in *Cratylus*, 384d.

the same thing when he remarked, "No demonstration can prove that any particular name means any particular thing."[5]

Put simply, names, in themselves, are meaningless. Names *point* to objects or ideas. But they're just not the same things as what they're pointing to. This is important to understand: our experiences of everything (and I mean *everything*) are completely dependent upon symbolism. That's simply the way God designed us. Every time you think, you're using symbols. Saint Augustine said, "No one uses words except as signs of something else."[6] No wonder one semiotician called man (and, no doubt, woman) "the symbol-using animal."[7]

Here's the one big takeaway: symbolism has monumental importance to God. In fact, your words (which always precede your actions) are so important that they will *all* be brought into judgment on Judgment Day. This is why Jesus himself said, "I tell you that men [and women too] will have to give account on the day of judgment for *every careless word* they have spoken. For by your words you will be acquitted, and by your words you will be condemned" (Matthew 12:36–37). So Judgment Day will go well for you (or not so well) depending on the very words you have used to direct your life. Taken together, those words symbolize to God what you have counted as important in your lifetime.

Our Personal Symbolic Reality

Certainly, we communicate in symbols. What's more, our very conception of *reality* itself is built from layers of symbols. Chandler puts it this way: "Reality is a *system* of signs."[8] Therefore, our entire human experience of reality is also *completely* symbolic. This is not to say that actual objects don't *exist*. It's just that our *experience* of them is all symbolic. If, for example, you place a lot of importance on (and get happiness from) your family and friends, then you will construct your reality in some part around those people you love. So reality for

---

[5]   Aristotle, "Posterior Analytics."
[6]   St. Augustin, *On Christian Doctrine*, I.2.2.
[7]   Chandler, "Signs," 2.299.
[8]   Chandler, "Introduction."

you is, in part, the sum of images and other sense perceptions in the form of mental symbols that make the most memorable impression on your mind. We all store these images in our brains and, theologians would argue, in our souls or spirits

Meaning occurs for us when we place special importance on *some* things and *certain* people more than we do on others. We assemble a network of various chosen experiences into a whole which then becomes our reality, our life experience. Chandler confirms this when he says, "Meaning is not 'transmitted' to us—we actively *create it* according to a complex interplay of codes or conventions of which we are normally unaware."[9]

God and the Meaning of Life

It shouldn't surprise us, then, that God wants to be an essential part of the meaning we build for ourselves. He makes himself known to us through language in the Bible, and through the vastness and power of creation. Psalm 19:1 says, "The heavens declare the glory of God. There is no speech or language where their voice is not heard." God is not silent in the universe, but it is up to us to value God as the One through whom all our experiences derive their meaning. If one asks, "What is the meaning of life?" the humanistic answer might be, "Meaning is the sum total of the most important experiences of each individual's life." But something is left out of that equation. Since we are made in God's image, every experience our mind processes has already passed through the filter of God's image within our human spirit, which he gave us at the time he created us. The most accurate and objective meaning of a person's life is created when they assign the proper value to experiences in their life, as seen through the eyes of our Creator. In other words, God comes first, then our experiences. The problem with creating our own meaning is that there are endless thousands of ideas and experiences to choose from, and being the sinners that we are, we don't always assign the same importance to an experience that God would. Again, meaning is something "we

---

[9] Chandler, 11.

actively create." If we don't keep God in mind as we process our experiences, God will never be the foundation of our reality and meaning, and that is right where Satan wants us. As the Psalmist wrote,

> The Lord looks down from heaven on the children of man, to see if there are any who understand, who seek after God. They have all turned aside; together they have become corrupt; there is none who does good, not even one. (Psalm 14:2, 3 ESV)

Even though God's nature and symbolic image are built directly into every human being, men and women are still free to ignore or even defy God, placing meaning and value on everything in life *except* God. It is only because we are made in the image of God that we have the freedom to deny the existence of God.

The devil wants us to pay no attention to the symbols God has made such as male-female distinctions or marriage in the sense of one man married to one woman. Once we are comfortable *without* God's intended meaning for mankind, Satan has us in his grip, often without our knowing it. Nonbelievers go through life, building symbol upon symbol, creating ever-deepening meaning, all without God. Fortunately for the believer, God indwells the Christian with his Spirit in order to give us a new way of thinking, one that honors and glorifies himself, and places man where he once was, below God in the "order of importance," teaching us to be sensitive to, and to properly judge, the symbolism all around us with God at the head of all creation.

Breaking God's Symbolism

When biblical symbols such as marriage are properly understood, they should help us understand God and motivate us to want to keep these symbols unbroken so that God is not offended by our behavior. When an individual rejects and violates the meaning behind a symbol, or when a government makes it easy for its citizens to break God's symbolism by legitimizing any form of sin such as adultery or homosexuality, Satan's grip on that individual or nation is strengthened, and God's kingdom is not advanced. Of course, there is forgiveness after a person sins against God, but the consequences are not so easily dismissed. God takes his laws and symbolism seriously, and so does Satan.

The Meaning of Life in Symbols

It all boils down to this: everything in our human experience is symbolic. Nineteenth-century philosopher Charles Peirce stated, "We [humans] think only in signs."[10] That's a remarkably sweeping statement to make about the human thought process and about human consciousness itself. It speaks volumes about what kind of creatures God has created, specifically creatures who should understand symbols, since we are utterly dependent on them. Symbolism is how we think, and it is how God thinks as well. He created us to communicate with himself, and the sooner we get familiar with symbols having the big Do Not Violate sign hanging on them, the sooner we can make peace with God and avoid the frustration of going hard against the currents of life and risk being spiritually lost by wrongly valuing *broken* symbols that violate God's character.

From what we have learned about symbolism, we can see that the entire business of giving meaning to the human race depends upon symbolism. We will see in later chapters how vital it was to understand and obey important symbols throughout Scripture and why breaking symbolism was often met with harsh punishment.

---

[10] Peirce, *Collected Papers of Charles Sanders Peirce*, 13.

2

How God Thinks

He who forms the mountains, creates the wind,
and reveals his thoughts to man…the LORD God
Almighty is his name.

—Amos 4:13

At least one ancient Greek thinker recognized the use of symbolism as the pinnacle of human thought. From what we see in Scripture, symbolism could very well be the pinnacle of God's thinking as well, at least as far as we can tell, given our very limited human understanding of God's metaphysical nature. The close of the Old Testament canon came around 430 BC, almost a thousand years after the death of Moses. Shortly after, during the 300's BC, Aristotle lived and gathered his own wisdom in ancient Greece by observing mankind and the natural world around him, much as Solomon did in Jerusalem some six hundred years before. One of the many books Aristotle wrote was his *Poetics*. There, Aristotle said it takes a genius to have a command of the use of metaphor,[11] yet another form of symbolism. Over three hundred years after Aristotle, and just days before his crucifixion, Jesus confronted the Jewish leaders who would soon arrest him, displaying his own genius in the use of metaphor to show how all men owe their devotion to God, every bit as much as they owed taxes to Caesar.

---

[11] Aristotle, *Poetics*.

The Genius of Metaphor

Metaphor, according to the Oxford English Dictionary, is

> the figure of speech in which a name or descrip-
> tive term is transferred to some object different
> from, but analogous to, that to which it is prop-
> erly applicable.[12]

Another dictionary gives the definition as "something used, or regarded as being used, to *represent something else*; emblem; symbol."[13] In both definitions there is the element of one thing referring to another, only now in a poetic context. As with other symbolism, the chief ingredients of metaphor are a signifier and the thing signified.

In his *Poetics,* Aristotle recognized the importance of metaphor. In chapter 22 of that work, he started a line of reasoning on how to have a command of poetic language in general. He began by stressing how important it was to be careful when employing literary conventions like the use of rare and unusual words. He wrote,

> It is a great matter to observe propriety in these
> several modes of expression, as in compound
> words, strange (or rare) words, and so forth.[14]

He then finished the thought with an explanation of the most compelling method of expression, that of the metaphor:

> *But the greatest thing by far is to have a command
> of metaphor.* This alone cannot be imparted by
> another; it is the mark of genius.[15]

---

[12] *Oxford English Dictionary* (1971), s.v. "metaphor."
[13] Dictionary.com, s.v. "metaphor, accessed January 19, 2012, emphasis mine.
[14] Poetics, chapter XXII.
[15] Poetics, ibid., emphasis mine.

What is it about having a command of metaphor that elevates a person (in Aristotle's mind, at least) to the level of genius? He provides this reason: "to make good metaphors implies an eye for resemblances."[16] It seems that the ability to draw resemblances or parallels between particular objects or ideas is the stuff that geniuses are made of. To create a metaphor, Aristotle gave an example. He chose two phrases, each with a subject and object, whose meanings had something in common—in this case, the passage of time.

> As old age is to life,
> so is evening to day.

He then takes the subject of each phrase and used it to modify the object of the opposite phrase. By making this twist, two new metaphors were born:

> Evening may therefore be called
> "the old age of the day,"
> and old age "the evening of life."[17]

This "eye for resemblances" and crafting associations between mostly different things is what Aristotle said defined a person as a genius.

Jesus as Defender of Symbolism

Jesus certainly had this eye for resemblances as well. During the Lord's last week before his death, he was confronted several times by the Pharisees, who wanted to arrest and kill him. He responded with a parable directed at them—another example of symbolism—which got them so angry that they "sent spies" to trap him, including some Herodians. The Pharisees hated Rome, but the Herodians loved Rome. Together they crafted a question so carefully that they

---

[16] Ibid.
[17] Ibid., chapter XXI.

knew they would trap Jesus no matter how he answered. They first complimented Jesus on how truthful and impartial he was. Then they dropped the bomb: "Is it lawful for us to give tribute to Caesar or not?"[18]

The challenge seemed unwinnable. Either way, Jesus would have to come out either for or against Rome, which could split his followers' opinion of him and would certainly make him an enemy of either Israel or Rome. Until that time, Jewish leaders were unable to arrest Jesus because the people were behind him. As Luke 20:19 tells us, "The teachers of the Law and the chief priests looked for a way to arrest him immediately... But they were afraid of the people." If he came out in favor of paying taxes to Caesar, that support could disappear at a moment when he was presenting himself to Israel as their Messiah since he had already made his triumphal entry into Jerusalem just days before. But if he came out against paying the tribute, the Jewish leaders could paint Jesus as just another rebel from Galilee, an area known for its zealots and rebels, which could lead to a most unpleasant uprising which Pontius Pilate would try at all costs to avoid.

One such rebel, Judas the Galilean, had incited the people to resist paying taxes some thirty-seven years earlier in an incident so devastating that the Jewish leaders and Jesus himself must certainly have been aware of it. This tax was imposed on Judea beginning around 4 BC.[19] Soon after, Judas the Galilean[20] (not the disciple) began to stir the pot of tax revolt,[21] appealing to the first commandment: "You shall have no other gods before Me."[22] Judas used this commandment as a prohibition against paying taxes to Rome so the people wouldn't have their allegiance to God divided. But Judas also

---

[18] Luke 20:22.

[19] Josephus's dating of 6AD is problematic. See support for the earlier date in Rhoads, J. H. (2011), Josephus Misdated the Census of Quirinius. *Journal of the Evangelical Theological Society*, 54.

[20] Acts 5:37.

[21] Myers, "Jewish Revolts."

[22] Exodus 20:3.

had ambitions to become king.[23] He captured the town of Sepphoris, the capital of Galilee, just four miles northwest of Nazareth. This prompted Varus, Rome's governor of Syria, to come down hard on Judas's rebellion. Varus crucified some two thousand people and sold another thirty thousand into slavery.[24] Sepphoris and hundreds of other towns were destroyed.

Paying tax to Rome was a deeply symbolic reminder of Israel's loss of freedom. There was no way Jesus would have been unaware of Judas the Galilean's revolt. As a builder's son, he may have even had a hand, along with his father, in the rebuilding of some of the destroyed villages, or even of Sepphoris itself, just an hour's walk from Nazareth. Being set up as a possible tax rebel so soon after the incident at Sepphoris is something the Lord would have seen coming a mile away.

Instead of walking into their trap, Jesus said, "Show me a denarius." Most likely, one of the Herodians had one handy. But producing it while standing on Temple property only proved their hypocrisy, especially because Roman law *allowed* the Jews to pay the tax with equivalent *copper* coins, which didn't have the offending image of Caesar.[25] The Lord continued, "Whose portrait and inscription are on it?" They replied, "Caesar's."[26] Then Jesus delivered a two-part metaphorical smack-down to the religious leaders, leaving their scheme in flames.

In considering the image of Caesar on a Roman coin, the Lord immediately identified Caesar's image as an icon of Caesar himself. This highlighted the responsibility of the people to give back a part of what rightfully belonged to Caesar. Jesus quickly drew the following parallel in his mind:

> As Caesar's image is on the coin
> So is God's image upon the man.

---

[23] Du Toit et al., *The New Testament Milieu*. Also, Josephus, *Antiquities*, 17.272.
[24] Durant, *Caesar and Christ*, 543.
[25] Ibid., 543.
[26] Luke 20:24–25a.

The Lord drew a quick conclusion from that metaphor:

> Caesar has power over the coin that bears *Caesar's* image, so God should also have power over the man bearing *God's* image.

If "genius" is the level of intellect required for a man to master the metaphor, then what should we say about Jesus, who *created* man to be a metaphor for God? Jesus was able to see the resemblance between two phrases that turn on the use of the word "image." He quickly drew the association that God's image was upon the man simply by looking at the image on the coin. Expertly employing this kind of symbolism over and over again in Scripture simply demonstrates that God thinks in symbols and that he is the original Genius over metaphor.

The reason Jesus had no problem with paying this tax is because Caesar could only be in power with God's permission. As he said later that week to Pontius Pilate, "You would have no power over me if it were not given to you from above."[27] God has the power and complete freedom to remove whatever king displeases him. So it follows that a king in power at any given time serves some purpose of God's. God is not threatened by having evil men in power. If God wants a king deposed, he can do it. Caesar had the power and authority to mint those coins with his own image on them. The image on those coins conveyed the power of Rome, including the power to collect taxes and the power to kill anyone who resisted. But the Lord Jesus wasn't done. He wasn't about to leave Caesar with all the power.

The second part of his answer also hit them right between the eyes. The Pharisees *and* the Herodians *and* Caesar were *all* stamped with God's image, so Jesus continued by adding,

> And [give] to God the things that are God's.[28]

---

[27] John 19:11.
[28] Luke 20:25c, *The Holy Bible: English Standard Version.*

Caesar had the right to demand the money that bore his image. But God had a greater right since *all people* bear the image of God. Therefore, every person is obliged to give of their money to human authorities, but you and I should also give our entire *being* to God, the highest authority and the One whose image we all bear.

God's Big Risk in Making Us in His Image

That God has a claim on every person who bears his image doesn't mean all would obey him. Subjects of Rome could choose to pay taxes to the Romans or not, so long as they were willing to accept the consequences if they disobeyed. Caesar had the power to take taxes by force if he so chose. God also has the right and the power (then and now) to take what he wants from people by force. But God never forces himself on us in this fashion because God desires *love* and a willing spirit from his creatures, and love must be freely given.[29] As Gregory Boyd explained in his *Satan and the Problem of Evil,* God could have created us in such a way that we had *no choice* but to love him. He even could have deceived us into thinking that this love came happily from our own free will. But if God were satisfied with that arrangement, wouldn't he be deceiving himself? Such "love" would leave him completely unfulfilled in his quest for our *real* love and devotion toward him.[30] Therefore, God gave us complete freedom in how we respond to his promptings, leaving open the possibility and risk that the individual will not love him in return.

The Battle for Meaning

Despite the limitless power of God, still he will not force us to accept him. He has chosen to wage his own battle against the power of Satan for the hearts and minds of men and women. Even the symbolism he has built into his creation falls prey to competing interpretations. Chandler confirms that symbols can be interpreted in many

---

[29] Boyd, *Satan and the Problem of Evil,* 53–87.
[30] Ibid, 55.

ways, even to the point that reality itself can be manipulated: "Realities are contested, and textual representations are thus 'sites of struggle.'"[31] This is exactly what was happening when the Lord spoke to the people in parables just before the confrontation over the denarius. Parables are yet another form of symbolic speech designed to hide their intended meaning. Jesus didn't mean to frustrate people with his use of parables; rather, he used them as bait. He wanted his listeners to struggle a little with their meaning, hoping to catch some of them. This was the way Jesus put into practice the very thing he told the disciples, that they, too, would become fishers of men. But he would only catch some. Jesus said to his disciples, "To you it has been given to know the secrets of the kingdom of God, but for others they are in parables, so that seeing they may not see, and hearing they may not understand." The people struggled to understand the meaning behind the parables with some able to understand and others giving up and calling Jesus "mad."

In the West, we are engaged at the present time in this strug-gle for meaning. Those people who don't have God as an important symbol in their construction of reality are fighting politically against those of us who do have God as our foundation. Millions have given up on Christianity, calling it a bunch of outdated and restrictive rules and regulations. But that was the furthest thing from what Jesus was trying to teach. He wanted an authentic and committed belief in God, one that would meet everyone's deepest spiritual needs. It's crucial that we maintain our Christian testimony to a dying world. God demands that we always keep him at the center of our think-ing and at the base of all our meaning in this present life. Consider how Moses commanded the Israelites to keep God in their thoughts before entering the Promised Land:

> Hear, O Israel: The LORD our God, the LORD is one. Love the LORD your God with all your heart and with all your soul and with all your strength. These commandments that I give you today are to be upon your hearts. Impress them on your

---

31 Chandler, 60.

children. Talk about them when you sit at home and when you walk along the road, when you lie down and when you get up. Tie them as symbols on your hands and bind them on your foreheads. Write them on the doorframes of your houses and on your gates.[32]

Since we live in New Testament times, we live by a higher standard—being controlled by God's Spirit—not by keeping the letter of the law of Moses. By living according to the Spirit, we can expect the blessing of God's presence. As Paul noted,

Those who live in accordance with the Spirit have their minds set on what the Spirit desires. The mind of sinful man is death, but the mind controlled by the Spirit is life and peace.[33]

We've seen that every thought, word, or action a person can make is somehow symbolic. If man is a "symbol-using animal,"[34] then God designed us that way, making him the symbol-designing Creator. So now we understand at least one way that God thinks. He might have ten million *other* ways of thinking that we cannot comprehend, but we at least know that he thinks symbolically, just as we do. Knowing a little about how God thinks can help us understand why God does what he does and where we go wrong when we act in ways that are contrary to his.

We have a responsibility to recognize the symbols God has planted in our world. Symbols can either be respected and followed or disrespected and broken. The next chapters will look at both.

---

[32] Deuteronomy 6:4–9.
[33] Romans 8:6.
[34] Chandler, *Collected Writings*, 1931–58.

3

Destroying the Image of God

> God created man in his own image... God saw
> all that he had made and it was very good.
>
> —Genesis 1:27, 31

> So, the Lord said, "I will wipe mankind, whom I
> have created, from the face of the earth...for I am
> grieved that I have made them."
>
> —Genesis 6:5–8

G od has placed certain aspects of his image into many areas of
creation. A created thing can't help but display aspects of its
creator. The six days of Genesis 1 where God created order from
chaos and created the variety of materials and living creatures, all in
amazing balance, shows how majestic his wisdom and knowledge
truly are. By creating man on the sixth day, God showed that mankind was the pinnacle of his creative work. Only in Adam and Eve
did God place his very own image, by breathing his Spirit into them,
and so they became symbolic of God himself:

> So, God created man in his own image,
> in the image of God he created him;
> male and female he created them.[35]

---

[35] Genesis 1:27.

The symbolic image of God was broken when Adam and Eve chose to obey Satan rather than the God whose image they bore. That started the long history of breaking the symbolism God designed into the world and brought the punishment resulting from breaking that symbolism.

Michelangelo, the Creator

To better understand how God feels about his image in mankind being defaced, consider the great Renaissance sculptor and artist Michelangelo. Two of his sculptures tell the story of both symbolism and broken symbolism. In ancient days, it was said that artists (especially sculptors) came about as close to God's act of creation as humans could conceivably come. Some liken sculpture to God's creating the soul within the human body. From his letters, Michelangelo described how he carved one of his images. He wrote, "I saw the angel in the marble and carved until I set him free."[36] To look at an irregular block of marble, see a beautiful work of art within, and then, with a hammer and chisel, break a masterpiece out of the rock is almost supernatural to those of us who know nothing about that craft.

The statue of David was one statue that had special patriotic meaning to Michelangelo because it was sculpted for his beloved Florence, which had recently renewed its status as a republic. Florence had been victorious in two earlier wars, one against Pisa in 1364, the other against Milan in 1440. Florence needed a symbol to confirm the spirit of victory in the minds of the people.[37] To Michelangelo, the ancient warrior-child David was that perfect symbol. In the Old Testament, David had defeated Goliath in hand-to-hand combat. The statue of David symbolized many things: strength of character, preparedness in the face of military threat, heroism, inner spiritual strength, and a warning to anyone who would rule over Florence.

---

[36] Diary, http://simplyknowledge.com/popular/biography/michelangelo, accessed July 17, 2019.

[37] Brucker, *Renaissance Florence*, 268–271.

Symonds commented on the emotion conveyed by the statue. He said,

> [David] first displayed that quality of *terribilità*, of spirit-quailing, awe-inspiring force, for which he afterward became so famous… The heroic boy, quite certain of victory, is excited by the coming contest. His brows are violently contracted, the nostrils tense and quivering, the eyes fixed keenly on the distant Philistine… The sling…is held with the left hand, poised upon the left shoulder, ready to be loosed.[38]

The statue of David was packed with symbolism, virtually bursting with the image that Michelangelo hoped would characterize Florence for years to come.

Michelangelo was so proud of this sculpture that he wanted to display it prominently. A committee was formed to discuss where to place the statue. This committee was comprised of other sculptors, wood-carvers, goldsmiths, and painters, including Botticelli and even Leonardo da Vinci.[39] Eventually, Michelangelo himself selected the Palazzo Vecchio as the place for the statue to stand, a place with great public visibility.

When it came time to move the statue, it took forty men to move it. According to one account, "they broke the wall above the gateway enough to let it pass."[40] A large wooden structure was built and placed upon wooden rollers. The statue was suspended inside the structure with ropes so it could swing freely as the vehicle crept forward, jarring and jerking its way along the rugged cobblestone road.[41] The record of moving the giant statue included an account of stones being thrown at it by vandals the first night of the journey. Symonds

---

[38] Symonds, *The Life of Michelangelo Buonarrot*, 62–63.
[39] Hughes, *Michelangelo*, 68.
[40] Symonds, 96.
[41] Ibid, 96.

writes, "That night some stones were thrown at the Colossus with intent to harm it."[42] Apparently, it escaped any damage. No doubt, Michelangelo would have been furious if any part of the masterpiece was harmed or its symbolism diminished. Instead, his pride grew with his legend at the completion of this masterpiece. After looking at his creation of man and all the universe, God concluded, "It is very good."[43] God does not get angry in this age because this or that law was broken. With him, it is much more about man ruining his own image. Man's image is God's image, and when God's image and plan for mankind is broken, he is deeply hurt and insulted. He is also vulnerable to the taunting of his immortal enemy, Satan.

The *Pietà* and Broken Symbolism

Michelangelo was clearly pleased with his sculpture of David and all the symbolism it represented, the perfect statue for a humanistic age. But Michelangelo was also vigorous in defending his work with a strong temper. Pope Julius II once said that Michelangelo "is terrible, as you see, one cannot get on with him."[44]

One day in Saint Peter's Cathedral, the famous sculptor overheard one visitor incorrectly tell another that the sculpture of Mary holding the dead body of Christ, Michelangelo's famous *Pietà*, was carved *not* by Michelangelo but by one of his acquaintances, a sculptor named Cristoforo Solari. Michelangelo poured much of his life and expertise into the sculpture, so the *Pietà* meant a great deal to him. The misidentification of the sculptor meant that the beauty of the work was attributed to someone else, and so did the prestige due to its creator. The beauty of his creation was torn from him. God feels the same way when *his* creation is attributed to, say, the undirected forces of matter in the universe, randomly producing the order and beauty of the world we live in.

From Michelangelo's point of view, attributing his work to someone else represented broken symbolism, just like Satan stealing the obedience

---

42 Ibid., 96.
43 Genesis 1:31
44 Symonds, 346–347.

and affection of Adam and Eve represented broken symbolism to God. Michelangelo was so incensed that someone else was getting credit for his masterpiece that he went back that night with hammer and chisel and, in Latin, carved into the sash draped across Mary's chest, "Michelangelo Buonarroti the Florentine Made This."[45] He later regretted doing it because he made himself a distraction to the beauty of the statue.

As the creator of the sculpture, he had the right and the freedom to identify the work however he pleased. Do you remember how God expressed regret after he brought the Flood upon the earth, killing all its inhabitants except for Noah and his family? God destroyed the beautiful work of his own hands because it had been defaced by Satan and his demon followers. Yet God now allows men and women in every age since the Flood to use their free will in any way they choose even though he created them and is fully deserving of their praise and honor. Michelangelo vowed to never sign another work of his hands. God also vowed never to destroy the earth again by flood. The rainbow is proof of that promise. Many who abuse God's creation have even taken the sign of the rainbow as their own symbol, waving their disobedience, as it were, in God's face. But after the Flood, God promised to overlook our willful, broken symbolism until that day of judgment in the future when we will all give account for our sins. Until then, we all benefit from his love and grace.

Whether it is God putting his image into Adam or a sculptor giving a soul to a block of marble, the artist's character can be seen in his creation. Those who seek to destroy the artist's image or attribute the work to the wrong person are sure to face the artist's wrath. Is it any wonder that, one day, God's temper will also flare after his own symbolic image in creation has been violated for so long by Satan and most of the human race? God has every right to be incensed.

Satan's Attack on the Master's Masterpiece

Satan has always been active behind the scenes, working feverishly to attack God's creation. During the time before the Flood,

---

"A Masterpiece Is Born," retrieved July 17, 2019.

demons mated with human females, producing hybrid beings known as Nephilim.[46] This irreparably harmed the image of God in human beings. The inhabitants of the earth became so polluted as to make them irredeemable in God's eyes—all except for the family of Noah. This is why God brought the Flood upon the earth. It is always Satan's plan to destroy the image of God in creation, wherever it is found.

God spoke to Noah when he emerged from the ark. He had good news and bad news. He said,

> Never again will I curse the ground because of man, even though every inclination of his heart is evil from childhood. And never again will I destroy all living creatures, as I have done.[47]

The good news was that God would never destroy man again no matter how sinful he was. The bad news is that God sees every human being as basically evil. All of us live with hearts full of evil inclinations—at least until we are born again by God's Spirit through the blood of Jesus. Sadly, those who turn away from God see themselves as basically good people. They don't see the danger they're in.

At some time in the future, he will swiftly bring to an end all sin worldwide—not with a flood but with fire—and retake the kingdom of earth for himself. The breaking of all God's symbolism will cease. As Peter wrote,

> But the day of the Lord will come like a thief. The heavens will disappear with a roar; the elements will be destroyed by fire, and the earth and everything in it will be laid bare.[48]

---

[46] Genesis 6:4.
[47] Genesis 8:21.
[48] 1 Peter 3:10.

Imagine God destroying the work of his own creative hands a *second* time, the same creation that was once called "very good" in Genesis 1:31.

The Broken Symbolism of Atheism in Science

Since the beginning of recorded history, Satan has filled the world with false religions and philosophies—even false science. Evolutionary theory can either be based in atheism or it can have God at its base, directing the evolutionary process. God also could have spoken everything into existence over the six days of creation—a more literal interpretation of Genesis 1 and 2. But the only theory of origins allowed in today's public schools is the atheistic form of evolution that leaves God completely out of the picture.

This atheism-based theory of evolution has no explanation to one of the biggest problems in biology: how did life originate from inorganic material?[49] Christians understand that God breathed his Spirit into the first living things, giving them the life force necessary to reproduce. But atheists credit evolution with creating life from lifeless matter—matter in motion, and we don't even know the origin of the matter or how it was put into motion.

This is broken symbolism at its worst. Jesus himself said, "I am the way the truth and the life. No one comes to the Father except through me."[50] God is life. Anything that violates this attribute of God constitutes a broken symbol that will draw God's displeasure and eventual punishment. This undiscovered mechanism of life from non-life requires the same faith that atheists accuse Christians of having, when they bring God as creator into the realm of science. This is much worse than misinformed art patrons attributing Michelangelo's *Pietà* to Cristoforo Solari. This is nothing short of attributing God's life force within all living things to undirected, random chance muta-

---

[49] See M. Behe's *Darwin's Black Box* (1996) on biological design; *The Privileged Planet* (2001) by G. Gonzales and J.W. Richards on cosmological design; and S. Meyer's *Signature in the Cell* (2009), p. 207, on the mathematical impossibility of creating even a single protein—essential to life—by random chance mutation.

[50] John 14:6.

tion acting on self-existing matter, without any purpose whatsoever. This theory might as well be called, *Life from Nothingness*.

Once truth has been discarded and its symbolism broken beyond repair, it's easier to understand how God could destroy his own creation. It may even explain the ferocity of God's wrath branded upon his Son on the cross, once the truth of his identity and mission was rejected by God's own people—the very fabric of broken symbolism.

Objects Devoted to Destruction

When Israel entered the Promised Land, God sometimes required them to destroy entire cities including people and all their belongings. These people were doing all the same evil things that people living before the Flood were doing. The Nephilim—offspring of demons and human females—were in the land once again. These peoples represented broken symbolism to God, and he wanted them to be devoted to destruction or completely destroyed by fire.[51] These devoted people and their belongings[52] represented a disturbing degree of evil to God. Destroying them gave God an important victory in his spiritual warfare against Satan. He no longer had to look at a heathen city, prospering in the Promised Land. Instead, he looked down and saw piles of burned rubble, symbolizing the *destruction* of evil. Sometimes, God told Israel to destroy every man, woman, and child, along with every building, wall, and house. The exception was that some—but not all—precious metals were kept, purified, and placed into the Lord's treasury.[53] Presumably, these metal objects would be passed through fire and waters of cleansing in order to purify them.[54] But any idols made of or covered in gold, silver, or other metal would be destroyed

---

[51] Hebrew *cherem yohoram; cherem,* "devoted thing"; *Yohoram* is a form of *charam* (*destroy*, verb form).

[52] Hebrew *cherem,* noun form. See Deuteronomy 7:26. Some devoted objects were *not* considered broken symbolism and therefore not devoted to destruction. Fields devoted to the Lord, for example, were given to the priests. (See Leviticus 27:21).

[53] Joshua 6:24.

[54] Numbers 31:21–23.

by burning them completely in fire. None of that precious or common metal would be reclaimed, purified, or put into the Lord's treasury.

There was also punishment for anyone caught taking to himself things devoted to destruction. After being found out, the person with devoted things in his possession would be destroyed by fire, along with his or her family. God was very serious about destroying evil.

The entire city of Jericho was one example of a city to be devoted to destruction. This was the first city in the Promised Land that God commanded Joshua to attack after Israel left the wilderness and crossed the Jordan river. The army was to destroy everything in the city, including men, women, children, animals, and all the plunder that would normally belong to the soldiers. This city, by the way, also had giants—the Nephilim—as residents, even though all the Nephilim from Noah's age had been destroyed in the flood. Apparently, other fallen angels, once again, produced offspring from human females—similar to what occurred in the pre-Flood era. No doubt, God wanted those Nephilim in Jericho destroyed. Other cities in the Promised Land also contained giants. The Israelites, all the way down to the time of King David (who killed the giant named Goliath), had to fight and eradicate these giants from the land.

No doubt, this idea of a city or people being devoted to destruction is why God intends to eventually destroy the entire planet by fire. Earth has become one great, big, broken symbol in God's mind. God also called items like gold and silver idols from captured heathen nations *devoted* things. These were to be destroyed because God said they were detestable to him. He warned the Israelites not to take such objects into their camps, or else their camps would also become detestable and liable to be destroyed.

The Amalekites were another people God targeted to be devoted to destruction. Because King Saul did not destroy every living thing in that city but kept the Amalekite king, sheep, and cattle alive, God, through the prophet Samuel, removed the kingship from Saul and his family and gave it to David instead. Sins that are sometimes small in our eyes are egregious in God's eyes. He desperately wants us to be separate from the world and its evil.

Western political and cultural leaders have led their nations far away from the Judeo-Christian moral foundation that they were founded upon. Since the sexual revolution of the 1960s and '70s, courts and politicians no longer consider sexual sins and perversions worthy of punishment even though some of these sins are also detestable in the eyes of God since they destroy both the image of God and (as we will see) the purpose and symbolism for which they were originally intended. Abortion, almost always the aftermath of sexual immorality, is considered murder by God but perfectly moral by progressives in Western nations.

God has a stake in how society develops through time, and ultimately, God must break through the noise to make sure his message gets out to every generation. Every passing year brings a new field of children to be seeded with God's message of salvation from sin through Christ. Each person must decide to follow the God of the Bible or reject the offer to have his or her sins forgiven. Everything is on the table with each new generation. God doesn't want any nation to abandon him altogether as they did at the Flood, at the Tower of Babel, or at other times in history. Sadly, the education of our children has become another playground for Satan. Schools that once started each day in prayer now ban the Bible and all religious speech lest someone become offended.

When a culture that once brought glory to God begins to abandon him, God sends warnings that can take many forms (and are themselves often symbolic in nature) that are designed to bring about repentance and a societal correction. Perhaps, today, God is saying to our cultural elite, "If you feel uncomfortable living side by side with the 'religion' of Christianity, to the point that you feel the need to remove it from public view whenever you can, maybe you would be more comfortable living side by side with worshipers of Allah, the god of Islam, who will not stand for being pushed into a corner?" Punishing symbolically is often how God punishes or disciplines nations that turn away from him. More on this later.

The teaching of evolution, if it is based in atheism, destroys the symbolic image of God because it deprives God of the glory due to him as Creator of the universe. Sexual immorality also symbolically defaces the faithfulness, purity, and pleasure that God designed into his relationship with mankind. Both sins have led to a devaluation of human life that will ultimately lead God, once again, to destroy his own creation. God will be justified, one day in the future, in bringing judgment on mankind and on Satan and his legions who have worked so diligently to seduce billions of men, women, and children to follow evil instead of good.

Insulting Someone Who Buys Paint by the Barrel

In his later years, Michelangelo's temper was once again directed against one of his critics. A man named Biagio da Cesena, master of ceremonies at the Vatican, spoke out against Michelangelo's liberal use of nudity in his painting of the Last Judgment, stating that it was fit for a pub or a public bathhouse, not for a church. He was quite right, as far as Judeo-Christian morality was concerned, but word had it that Biagio had an illegitimate daughter of his own.[55] So Michelangelo rewarded Biagio by painting him into the Final Judgment in the ceiling of the Sistine Chapel, in the depths of hell, with donkey ears and a serpent coiled twice around him, biting him in the private parts as demons looked on.[56]

The point: Michelangelo was jealous of his masterpieces and wasn't afraid of punishing those who criticized him. He even felt justified sending someone to hell, figuratively speaking, at least. None of us enjoys being criticized, so at that level, we can understand his anger. Criticizing a serious artist's work is like thrusting a sword into his very soul. His work was his life. What he portrayed were the ideas he felt most deeply about. When an artist executes a serious piece, he's the judge of all the world—or at least of his own world. Likewise, when words are not enough to express our deepest feelings, we depend on symbols, often in art or music, to embody those sentiments.

---

[55] Steinberg, Michelangelo's Painting: Selected Essays, 169.
[56] Goldscheider, Michelangelo: Paintings, Sculpture, Architecture, 32.

We should be able to understand, therefore, why broken symbols greatly offend God, the architect of creation, and the symbolism behind it, where the cost is much higher than a bruised ego. Of course, what offends God and what offends Michelangelo are worlds apart. God created man in God's own image. Therefore, anyone violating man's image also violates God's and runs the risk of literally, not figuratively, going to hell. If we begin with choosing to love God rather than his enemy, we will begin to understand how God thinks. Then we can make it our own desire not to offend him, the same way as we would in any love relationship.

Satan wants just the opposite, promising pleasure while hiding the fact that there is punishment for choosing against God, followed by eternal judgment. Satan is a liar and always seeks to turn us away from God. God is a loving God, but he is also a warrior God. He will punish his enemies one day but not out of pride, pleasure, or to angrily uphold his own reputation as did Michelangelo. God will have his day of victory. But as is always the case with broken symbolism, it will be a bitter victory.

4

Divine Drama

God pleads obedience from us,
That he might take us to the stage
And perform his loving drama with us.
In view of all the world
Will he shower his love and anguish upon us…

—the author

S o far, we have considered man-made signs like Valentine hearts
and how the Lord Jesus defended the image of God in man.
We've also looked at how God made everything in our experience to
be symbolic, in one way or another. We've also explored metaphors
and parables that make comparisons between two mostly different
objects or ideas and showing God to be the genius that he is. There
is yet another more mysterious dimension to symbolism, where God
sets up a human drama, as if in a theater, to demonstrate some aspect
of his character or to foreshadow a coming event. This is God at his
best. For him, all the world's a stage! It's a kind of symbolic acting
in Scripture that sometimes got really wild and drove religious leaders and those unconcerned with God to near hysteria because they
often couldn't understand the symbolism of what they were watching. However, when they did grasp it, the slam was often against
them. Such signs were acted out by patriarchs, prophets, and by Jesus
himself before peasants, Pharisees, and kings.

This kind of drama is also God at his most terrifying. God's punishment against the apple of his eye, Israel, came twice before the arrival of Jesus: once in response to their unbelief before entering the Promised Land, and again after they turned to gross idolatry while in the Land, resulting in God's sending the Jews away in disgrace, some to Assyria, others to Babylon. All such symbols are carefully designed by God. It's from this kind of play-acting we learn that, when God chooses to punish for misbehaving, he even builds symbolism into the punishment for his people to understand their actions from his point of view. It's a kind of "this is how it feels to be me" lesson from God to those he truly cares deeply about. He wants to see a reaction from believers and nonbelievers alike—*any* reaction. It's as if God is taking our pulse to see if there's any life in us at all.

God thinks in all kinds of signs. In fact, God uses symbolism throughout the Bible. He even puts his reputation on the line with some of the most extreme, sometimes bizarre symbols ever recorded (including many sexual ones). He also dispenses some of the harshest, seemingly disproportionate penalties given for breaking what an average person might consider symbols of only scant importance. But to God, these symbols aren't empty or just for show. God takes seriously the symbols he has made—life-and-death seriously. King David wrote, "Kiss the Son, lest he be angry, and you be *destroyed* in your way"[57] (see 1 Sam 10:1 and 1 Kings 19:18). This is not a kiss of affection but of loyalty, showing respect to power. Those who choose not to respect the Son perish, so this kiss has very powerful symbolism behind it. In that sense, Judas's kiss used to betray Jesus was definitely *broken* symbolism. When Jesus came and revealed truth to the human race about God, he expected us to pay attention. There are grave consequences for ignoring or misinterpreting the signs God has left for us.

Abraham and the Death of a Son

Let's pretend for a moment that an older man who had no children was walking down the busy streets of New York. Suddenly another

---

[57] Psalm 2:12a.

man claiming to be a prophet appeared to the first man. This prophet appeared to the man from time to time giving him instructions and making some rather wild predictions. There was something about this prophet's character that caused the man to believe him and to obey what he said. On one occasion the prophet told the man he would soon have a son. Within a year that prediction came true. This prophet then appeared to the man one more time. This time, the prophet revealed that he was, in fact, God. The man thought to himself, *He might very well be God. After all, who can predict the future like this guy? And I've never felt this kind of love and good fortune before.* If this prophet, now known to be God, then told the man to take his son to Central Park and offer him there upon a certain rock *as a sacrifice*, what would that man do? Would he not change his mind immediately about the prophet's claim to be God, instead believing he was an imposter and an evil predator? It would make no sense at all to believe such a person.

Someone in the modern world who honestly doesn't believe in God, has only their own judgment to rely on. They have no guarantee of an afterlife or knowledge that our consciousness is really our eternal human spirit that will live on forever after death. Even for someone who has had a life-changing encounter with the true God, being asked to violently kill your own child would be a bridge that even true believers might not want to cross, whether God commanded it or not. Yet, sacrificing his son on Mount Moriah is exactly what God told Abraham to do. If you were Abraham, wouldn't that sound like an outrageous request? Even though God had a good reason for it, he didn't tell it to Abraham. Since Abraham seemingly had no good reason to obey, *why did he*? Wouldn't future generations look back at this story and call this "voice" claiming to be God nothing more than a lunatic hiding somewhere out of sight?" Abraham trusted God because God appeared and spoke to Abraham on several occasions *before* asking him to sacrifice his son. During these interactions with God, Abraham learned about God's character, and knew God was reliable. No one judging Abraham from outside could convince him that God was a deceiver. Why? Because *Abraham knew God*. What God was doing with Abraham and Isaac was deeply symbolic. In this case, the Lord was setting up one of those theatric dramas to get everybody's attention, one that would have obvious meaning for many generations to come, and a symbol that God definitely did not want broken.

When God asked Abraham to do something against human wisdom, Abraham obeyed without question. The logical consequence of knowing God personally (as Abraham did) is to do what he says. The Lord Jesus once said, "Why do you call me, 'Lord, Lord,' and do not do what I say?"[58] And so Abraham, when confronted by the voice of God, took his son to Mount Moriah as he was told.

Genesis 22 records the account of God involving Abraham in the test of a lifetime. Here was the challenge presented to him:

> Sometime later God tested Abraham. He said to him, "Abraham!"
>
> "Here I am," he replied.
>
> Then God said, "Take your son, your only son, Isaac, whom you love, and go to the region of Moriah. Sacrifice him there as a burnt offering on one of the mountains I will tell you about."[59]

There are some interesting points made by VP Hamilton about the story itself.[60] First, it is a narrator telling the story about Abraham. When the narrator uses the name *God*, he precedes it with the definite article *the*. This he does in verses 1, 3, and 9. This is very likely done for emphasis. *The God* distinguishes the subject from any of the other gods of the day, which were indeed numerous. It also emphasizes the fact that it was the true God who actually spoke, and not something Abraham made up in his own version of reality. Even more interesting is the word order of verse 1. Although it may sound unusual to us, the usual word order in Hebrew would be, "Tested,

[58] John 6:46
[59] Genesis 22:1–2.
[60] Hamilton, *The Book of Genesis, Chapters 18–50*, Genesis 22.

Elohim Abraham" with the verb preceding the subject, as opposed to the common English word order, "*Elohim* tested Abraham." (*Elohim* being the Hebrew word used here for "God"). But in Genesis 22:1, the word order is switched. In this verse, the subject actually *precedes* the verb for added emphasis in the Hebrew, just like the word order in English. In addition, since the pronoun *he* is included in the Hebrew verb, the phrase comes out like this: "The *Elohim*—he tested Abraham!"[61] Again, this was done for added emphasis. Hamilton points out that this is known as a *"casus pendens."*[62] Another telling phrase that was lost in translation is the command *Take your son, your only son Isaac whom you love...* This sounds like the command of an authoritarian despot, taunting and even threatening Abraham, when actually the phrase in Hebrew is more like a plea, something like this: "Take, I beg you, your son, your only son Isaac whom you love."[63] The Hebrew particle—*no* is untranslated in most English versions (meaning it doesn't appear in the English Bible at all) but carries the meaning, "please," or "I beg you." Says Hamilton,

> [The particle] is used only five times in the entire OT [Old Testament] when God speaks to a person. Each time God asks the individual to do something staggering, something that defies rational explanation or understanding. Here then is an inkling at least that God is fully aware of the magnitude of his test for Abraham.[64]

This is reminiscent of Jesus telling the disciples to get into the boat, knowing that a storm was going to overtake them. Jesus actually *implored* the disciples to get into the boat.[65] He did this because

---

[61] Ibid., Genesis 22.
[62] Another example of this Hebrew construction would be, "The God of the Hebrews, he has created the world." Retrieved from http://www.dailyhebrew.com/glossary/ on February 25, 2012.
[63] Hamilton, The Book of Genesis, Chapters 18–50, Genesis 22.
[64] Hamilton, ibid.
[65] Matthew 8:18.

he knew he had an important lesson for the disciples to learn and he didn't want them to miss it. This emphasis is placed by God on symbols which have important meaning.

Far from being the request of an insane God-imposter, this account of Abraham and Isaac is a work of genius because of its metaphorical content, foreshadowing the death of the Son of God at the hand of his Father, who was offering the Son as a substitutionary payment for *our* sin.

A Modern Thinker's Response to Abraham's Faith

As Christians, Jews or even Muslims, we cheer Abraham for his immense faith and appreciate the sensitivity shown by God in the Hebrew text of this story. But to a non-believer looking at the story from a distance, this is still, on its face, perhaps the most bizarre divine request ever made to any human being. Looking only from a human point of view, it just doesn't make sense. The French existentialist Jean-Paul Sartre (1905–1980) reflected on what *he* would have done, had he been subjected to the same proposal. Sartre claims he would have asked himself, "Is it really an angel [making the request] and am I really Abraham? What proof do I have?"[66] In Sartre's mind, it seemed to make no difference whatsoever who was making the request. No one had the right to tell Abraham to kill his son, not even God himself. Sartre tells a story to bolster his case. He wrote:

> There was a madwoman who had hallucinations; someone used to speak to her on the telephone and give her orders. Her doctor asked her, "Who is it who talks to you?" She answered, "He says it's God." What proof did she really have that it was God? If an angel comes to me, what proof is there that it's an angel? And if I hear voices, what proof is there that they come from heaven and not from hell, or from the subconscious, or

---

[66] Sartre, *Being and Nothingness*, 32.

a pathological condition? What proves that they are addressed to me? What proof is there that I have been appointed to impose my choice and my conception of man on humanity? I'll never find any proof or sign to convince me of that.[67]

A defender of Sartre might respond that he was just trying to avoid acting in bad faith, but the Bible records that God spoke to and appeared to Abraham on several occasions. This was enough for Abraham to judge that it was truly God leading him. Judeo-Christian belief demands that we recognize when God is speaking to us and that we act accordingly, by faith. At God's command, Abraham, who was then known as Abram, left his father's house in what is now southern Iraq. He set out for Canaan, a land over 800 miles away, which he had never seen before. This took great faith in God.

By the time God commanded Abraham to offer his son as a burnt offering, Abraham knew God and believed that God was faithful enough that, if killing his son was what God wanted him to do, it was good enough for him. There was another thought in Abraham's mind which both intrigued him and gave him hope. Earlier in his life, God told the young Abram that his offspring through his son, Isaac would be like the stars in the sky[68], a promise that had not yet been fulfilled. If God allowed Isaac to be killed, that God would also have to raise him from the dead in order to make good on that promise. It is recorded there in Genesis 15 that "Abram believed the Lord, and he credited it to him as righteousness." This was a truly astonishing faith that Abram showed toward God. Søren Kierkegaard came up with a term for this kind of faith: *the teleological suspension of the ethical.* It basically means that if God gives you a command backed up by some purpose of his, then throw away every idea you ever had about what's ethical, and *obey God.*

The most important feature of this account of Abraham is the significance and symbolism, not only the foreshadowing of God the

---

[67] Gould and Truitt, 32.
[68] Genesis 15:4–6.

Father killing his Son, but also of *where* this incident took place. The only other mention of "Moriah" in the Bible is in 2 Chronicles 3:1, where on Mount Moriah, Solomon built his temple to the God of Israel. This is the place where King David saw the angel of the Lord standing, about to destroy Jerusalem with a plague because of David's unbelief. The Lord told David to build an altar there, and when he did, the plague stopped. Later, David directed Solomon to build the temple on the exact same spot, where an angel defended that holy place. In that temple was the most holy place, the place where the High Priest took the blood of the sacrifice each year and anointed the mercy seat atop the ark of the covenant. God himself was present between the wings of the golden cherubim which hovered above the ark. So the place where Isaac's blood would have been shed is the exact same place where the blood of the sacrifice would be poured out on the altar over a thousand years later. Do you think that *maybe* the Father wanted the blood of Jesus to be offered there on Mount Moriah as well? More on that to follow.

Sartre's response to this episode was one of doubt, not faith. His experience of God's command would have led to inaction rather than obedience. Had Abraham broken faith (as Sartre would have) and not gone through with this amazing spectacle, it would have symbolized God as the reticent Father, not willing to sacrifice his Son. The consequence to those coming to faith in the God of Israel could have been catastrophic. Knowing how Satan can turn human failures into his victory is an indication of how human history would likely have been impacted. Of course, in addition to the lessons God was teaching Abraham, God was also showing in symbolism that God really did have a Son (something many Jews deny to this day) and that God planned to offer him as a sacrifice for sin, just as God demanded an animal sacrifice for sin in times prior to the coming of the Messiah. The grief Abraham was feeling before plunging the knife was the same grief (in symbolism) that God would one day feel as he offered up his son, Jesus, who also obediently performed every task his Father asked of him. If you want to know how God felt when Jesus was on the cross, you need look no further than how Abraham must have felt on the way to Mount Moriah.

5

Moses Breaking Bad

The Lord said to Moses, 'Speak to that rock…
and it will pour out its water…' Then Moses
raised his arm and struck the rock twice with his
staff.

Near the End of the Wilderness Journey
Numbers 20:7–8, 11

M oses was guilty of breaking a highly important symbol, this
time involving the future of Israel and God's relationship to
mankind. Had God not punished Moses in a very public way, the
entire plan of God to lead Israel into the Promised Land may have
been jeopardized. The Israelites may have believed that future victory
over the Canaanites was achieved through human anger and strength.
Some key identifiers of the future Messiah would also have been mis-
understood. God could not let that possibility stand. Moses learned
a bitter lesson regarding breaking symbols that God designed for his
audience. Remember, God made man to be "symbol processors" with
God himself as the Master Symbol Designer. Whenever a major symbol is broken, there will always be consequences for the one breaking
the symbol. There are also consequences for God, including taunting
and insults from his enemy, Satan, and that may necessitate a change
of plans God may have had in mind for the future.

The Uncompassionate God?

It's all too common for human beings to question what they perceive as God's harsh actions on the one hand or God's complete inaction toward injustice on the other. They think he's too harsh, too forgiving, too fast, or too slow. God just can't get it right, but over and over again, in the pages of Scripture, God is shown to have good reason for the trials and tribulations appointed for his people. Even so, God knows how weak we are:

> As a father has compassion on his children,
> so the Lord has compassion on those who fear him;
> for he knows how we are formed,
> he remembers that we are dust...[69]

The truth is, no matter how dedicated the believer, when the trials come, we still sometimes act in unbelief by accusing the Lord of being too harsh and uncompassionate, if not outright negligent. This gives Satan the right to accuse us before the Father. Understanding that God may have an important purpose wrapped up in symbolism *should* have the effect on us of patiently waiting just a bit longer for an answer to our suffering. We know that God always has good purposes toward those who love him. Moses is one who wishes he had been a little more patient and obedient to God's commands.

Wandering Without Water

After the Exodus from Egypt (around 1450 BC), God led Israel through what some explorers and archaeologists now believe may have been northwestern Saudi Arabia, rather than the traditional site of the Egyptian Sinai Peninsula. Evidence for the Arabian view seems to abound.[70] The Exodus account tells of the Israelites, early in their

---

[69] Psalm 103:13.

[70] See an introduction to the evidence supporting the Northwest Saudi Arabia site for Mt. Sinai, the split rock and the wilderness journey of Israel at www.splitrockresearch.org.

journey, complaining bitterly to Moses that there was no water to drink. In this desert, which can reach temperatures over 120 degrees Fahrenheit, that's serious stuff. A person can only last a few days without water in that kind of heat. Moses went to God in prayer. God answered him, saying,

> Walk on ahead of the people. Take with you some of the elders of Israel and take in your hand the staff with which you struck the Nile and go. I will stand there before you by the rock at Horeb. *Strike the rock*, and water will come out of it for the people to drink.[71]

Notice that in this story, which took place in the beginning of Israel's wilderness journey at a place called Rephidim, God really did tell Moses to strike the rock with the staff he used in Egypt. This very rock is believed to have been found today in northwestern Saudi Arabia. There are pictures of it that show a tall, statue-like rock standing upright at the top of a hill, split from top to bottom.[72] The hill is rocky all around except for the area immediately below this split rock, which has been smoothed out by *something*. Could it have been done by water gushing forth from the rock for an extended period of time? Lord only knows, but after being told to strike the rock, Moses followed God's instructions and the water came pouring out as promised and everyone's thirst was relieved. That water provided for over a million people for almost a year. What Moses didn't know at the time was that the apostle Paul would later discuss these events and conclude that the rock was also a symbol, a metaphor that God used to represent the fact that Jesus, after he himself was struck,

---

[71] Exodus 17:5–6, emphasis mine.
[72] http://splitrockresearch.org/content/100/Field_Reports/The_Split_Rock, retrieved August 01, 2016.

would be the source of spiritual refreshment for believers just as that rock refreshed the thirst of the Israelites in the desert. Paul wrote:

> They all ate the same spiritual food and drank the same spiritual drink; for they drank from the spiritual rock that accompanied them, and *that rock was Christ.* Nevertheless, God was not pleased with most of them; their bodies were scattered over the desert. Now these things occurred as examples to keep us from setting our hearts on evil things as they did.[73]

So far, so good. Moses did the right thing. The rock, which is the type of Christ that God was setting up for future generations, still had its symbolism intact. The fact that Moses struck the rock indicated that the Messiah would have to be struck in order to bring spiritual refreshment to the people who needed living water from him. Remember the words the Lord Jesus spoke about this in John 7? They tell us that we as believers can have the same living water that flowed through Jesus the Rock flowing through us as well.

> On the last day of the feast, the great day, Jesus stood up and cried out, "If anyone thirsts, let him come to me and drink. Whoever believes in me, as the Scripture has said, 'Out of his heart will flow rivers of living water.'"[74]

What a promise! Striking the rock and having water flow out in a desert to meet the desperate needs of people whose lives hung in the balance—a beautiful symbol designed by God and executed by his servant Moses. The fulfillment in Jesus providing the living waters of salvation for equally desperate people was even more glorious. As

---

[73] 1 Corinthians 10:3–6.
[74] John 7:37–38, ESV.

Paul said, these symbols are useful to us, to help us understand God and walk more closely to him. The very next verse in John 7 says:

> "Now this he said about the Spirit, whom those who believed in him were to receive, for as yet the Spirit had not been given, because Jesus was not yet glorified."[75]

So these "living waters" actually symbolized the Holy Spirit flowing through a believer just as the water flowed out of the rock and into the mouths of thirsty followers. Other verses can also be found in the Old Testament which Jesus prophetically fulfilled because of his completed work of salvation:

- Isaiah 12:3: "With joy you will draw water from the wells of salvation" (ESV).
- Isaiah 44:3: "For I will pour water on the thirsty land, and streams on the dry ground; I will pour my Spirit upon your offspring, and my blessing on your descendants" (ESV).
- Joel 2:28: "And it shall come to pass afterward, that I will pour out my Spirit on all flesh; your sons and your daughters shall prophesy, your old men shall dream dreams, and your young men shall see visions" (ESV).

As Christians, we can experience this life in the Spirit. We do this by learning to "live by the Spirit" (Galatians 5:16). In a following verse, Paul also wrote, "Since we live by the Spirit, let us keep in step with the Spirit" (v.25). Paul in Romans 8 also tells us that living by the Spirit allows us to live lives that please God and, the Spirit also gives us the power to do that which the law of Moses never had the power to do. This power of the Spirit in us is the "living water" symbolized by Moses striking the rock in the desert causing the waters to gush out, and the fulfillment of this symbol by the Lord Jesus in

---

[75] John 7:39, ESV.

his death and resurrection helps us understand more about life in the Spirit and vice-versa, because *God thinks in symbols.*

Water from the Rock—Take 2

After that episode and the year-long stay at Mount Sinai, the people of Israel were led by God northward toward the Promised Land where Moses sent spies to spy out the land. Then, after refusing to take the next step and invade the land that God was giving them, Israel complained bitterly and told each other "we should choose a leader and go back to Egypt."[76] God was incensed at the unbelief of Israel. If God could spare them from the Egyptian army, he could certainly give them victory over the Canaanites. So God told Moses, "I will strike them down with a plague and destroy them, but I will make you into a nation greater and stronger than they."[77] But Moses interceded for Israel saying,

> If you put these people to death all at one time, the nations who have heard this report about you will say, 'The LORD was not able to bring these people into the land he promised them on oath; so he slaughtered them in the desert.'[78]

Then Moses pleaded further, reminding God what he said to Moses on Mt. Sinai:

> 'The Lord is slow to anger, abounding in love and forgiving sin and rebellion. Yet he does not leave the guilty unpunished; he punishes the children for the sin of the fathers to the third and fourth generation.' In accordance with your great love, forgive the sin of these people, just as you have pardoned them from the time they left Egypt until now.[79]

---

[76] Numbers 14:4.

[77] v. 12.

[78] v. 16.

[79] Numbers 14:18–19.

Moses won the argument and God forgave Israel for their complaining. But God also punished Israel in a symbolic way. God told Moses to pronounce judgment on all the Israelites, 20 years old or older, except for Joshua and Caleb, who took God at his word and were not afraid to go up against the Canaanites. God said thru Moses:

> As surely as I live, declares the LORD, I will do
> to you the very things I heard you say: In this
> desert your bodies will fall—every one of you
> twenty years old or more who…has grumbled
> against me. Not one of you will enter the land
> I swore with uplifted hand to make your home,
> except Caleb son of Jephunneh and Joshua son
> of Nun.[80]

God often punishes symbolically. In this case, the thing Israel feared came upon them, but only because of their unbelief. It didn't have to end that way. God made them wander through the wilderness in their unbelief until everyone in that disobedient generation had died. Only their children would enter the Promised Land.

Fast-forward about thirty-eight years or so.[81] Near the end of that journey, God led the new generation of Israelites to a place called Kadesh, an area where a similar story of Israel's suffering from thirst took place. (It seems this is a different place from where the rock was first struck further south in Rephidim, nearer to Mt. Sinai). It must have been an important lesson in God's mind for him to want to teach the same story about the rock to this new generation of Israelites.

Just as God pressed the original travelers many years before, this new generation also suffered from the same heat and thirst as they neared the end of their travels. The people began to lay into Moses again for taking them away from Egypt where water was plentiful. By

---

[80] vss. 28–30.

[81] An alternate view states that Israel arrived at Kadesh and then stayed there for thirty-eight years rather than wandering around the wilderness. See details at http://www.bible.ca/archeology/bible-archeology-exodus-route-sinai-kadesh-barnea.htm#thirtyeight. Also see Deuteronomy 1:46.

this time, he had been leading the people of Israel through the Sinai desert for nearly 40 years. God, never one to miss a complaint when it involved his oversight of Israel, wanted to build on the symbol Moses had already demonstrated once before. They didn't know it, but the symbol foreshadowed the Messiah to the Israelites. To set it up for maximum impact, God said to Moses,

> Take the staff, and you and your brother Aaron gather the assembly together. *Speak* to that rock before their eyes and it will pour out its water. You will bring water out of the rock for the community so they and their livestock can drink.[82]

Here's what happened next in Numbers 20:9–11:

1. Moses took the staff from the Lord's presence, just as he commanded him (v. 9)—okay so far.
2. He and Aaron gathered the assembly together in front of the rock (v.10)—again, okay so far.
3. Moses said to them, "Listen, you rebels, must we bring you water out of this rock?" (v.10)—careful, Moses! Don't give way to anger.
4. Then Moses raised his arm and struck the rock twice with his staff (v.11)—Oh no! Moses totally lost it and broke God's symbol by striking the rock instead of speaking to it.

Punishment for Breaking the Symbol

Understandably, Moses had grown weary of the complaints of the people. Rather than obey God (who had a quite specific reason for asking Moses to *speak* to the rock the second time), he instead *struck* the rock with his staff, just as he had done nearly forty years earlier (though twice this time). As we saw from the Apostle Paul's comments, this rock was still a representation of Jesus, the Messiah.

---

[82] Numbers 20:8, emphasis mine.

Moses already struck the rock once before, and God's intention was to leave it that way, since Christ was only meant to be struck one time for our sins. From that point onward, Jesus only needed to be *asked* to have the living waters of the Spirit poured out on the person requesting it. This reminds us of the time Jesus spoke to the woman at the well. He said to her, "If you knew the gift of God and who it is that asks you for a drink, you would have asked him and he would have given you living water."[83] Jesus was never to be struck again. So Moses destroyed the symbolism that God intended people of future generations to understand.

Let's look at this from Moses' point of view. For all the years of leading Israel, Moses put up with their constant complaints. He took their demands before God. He was forced to assert himself against those who would overthrow him. He begged God for forgiveness on behalf of the people when they disobeyed him. He even put some to death who refused to obey God's commands. He constantly carried all the day-to-day decisions on his shoulders for a people whose population may well have been over two million. And he did it for forty long years in 120+ degree desert heat. After all that, Israel came again to another rock in the desert where all were tired and thirsty. God told Moses this time to *speak* to the rock. But when that same Moses—who endured Israel for all those years—disobeyed God's command *just one time* by hitting the rock—just like he did on a previous occasion—what was his reward for all those years of dedicated service? He was reprimanded by God with these words:

> "Because you did not trust in me enough to honor me as holy in the sight of the Israelites, *you will not bring this community into the land I give them.*" These were the waters of Meribah,[84] where the Israelites quarreled with the Lord and where he showed himself holy among them.[85]

---

[83] John 4:10.
[84] *Meribah* means "quarreling."
[85] Numbers 20:12–13.

From Moses' point of view, this punishment must have been nothing short of devastating. He would never see the land he had been leading all of Israel toward for forty years. He would never see the victory over God's enemies, or the rest God promised for his people. The disappointment and rejection Moses felt must have been unbearable. However, God was laying down prophecy and symbolism for future generations. The writer of Hebrews pointed out:

> Moses was faithful as a servant in all God's house,
> testifying to what would be said in the future.[86]

Keeping symbolism intact was a matter of holiness that demanded nothing short of strict obedience. Breaking that symbol dishonored God and set a dangerous precedent in the people's eyes because rebellion can be contagious. Receiving the proper honor from those who pledge themselves to your service is important when you have enemies constantly trying to destroy the work of your hands.

Satan is always looking for ways to undermine God's plans. That's just who Satan is. In a military setting, being dishonored by your own soldiers in the face of battle can undermine the entire campaign and give victory to the enemy. Make no mistake, this was all-out war against Satan's stronghold in Canaan, the Promised Land given to Abraham some seven hundred years earlier. Remember that Satan's enterprise of making all the heathens of the earth give money, sacrifices, and even their own children to demon powers who controlled all the land that God promised to Israel, was an enterprise that God hated and wanted to win back through an obedient Israel. If God's most trusted servant, Moses, was unwilling to perform God's exact will by disobeying a direct order, Satan, no doubt, laughed in God's face, pointing to all the obedient souls he owned in Canaan, God's back yard.

Due to his disobedience, God denied Moses entry into the very Promised Land which he had waited all those long years to see with his own eyes. Is it possible that Satan had accused God of injustice by

---

[86] Hebrews 3:5.

continuing to reward a disobedient Moses with a trip to the Promised Land even after he broke God's symbolism? Remember how Satan accused God of protecting Job from harm and loss in the opening chapters of Job? God, willing to test Job's faithfulness, allowed Satan to attack all the blessings that God had given him. This is how Satan operates as he accuses us before the Father. First, Satan tempts us to sin. Then, after we sin, Satan goes to God and accuses us of doing exactly what he tempted us to do.

Could the test of Moses have been a similar kind of contest between Satan and God to see how faithful God's servants are to their Master? We don't know for certain, but it seems very possible. In fact, the struggle between Satan and Michael the Archangel, recorded in Jude verse 9, seems to indicate that there was a spiritual battle going on surrounding the body of Moses. Some say that Satan had a claim on Moses's body due to Moses murdering the Egyptian[87]. It might also be due to Moses' open defiance of God when he struck the rock twice. That action may have brought into question Moses' own salvation, leaving Satan an opening to claim Moses' body, and perhaps his very soul. There is no doubt that, at the time of his death, Moses was the center of attention, with many angelic observers waiting to see (and Satan himself arguing *against*) an honorable burial for Moses' body. In the end, Moses *was* honorably buried, and God proved himself holy and just in denying Moses the reward of entering the Promised Land.

Isn't it terrifying that Satan would want to drag into hell a servant of God of the caliber of Moses? Be warned: Satan would take us all down if he could.

If Moses had obeyed God, his obedience might have given much needed courage to the new generations of Israelites who *would* be going in to take the Land. The first city Israel was to take was Jericho. How were they supposed to take it? Simply by shouting on the seventh day after walking around it without speaking or shouting each day for the first six. There was no need to strike *anything* or to depend on their own strength in order to gain the victory God

---

[87] From the Assumption of Moses

wanted to give them. They only had to have faith and courage. Seeing Moses *speak* to the Rock may have been just the thing to bolster their confidence in taking Jericho and perhaps prevent further grumbling, which God always detested.

Editing Out God from the Script

Moses was certainly devastated at the punishment God pronounced on him for his disobedience. Sure, Moses had been angry, probably wanted to show a little bravado in striking the rock, to send a message that even though the people had the numbers, he still had the power, and he had the staff that parted the waters to prove it. But God had other ideas that he wanted Israel to comprehend when Moses would speak to the rock.

No doubt the generation now witnessing Moses at the rock that gushed with water had either witnessed the previous encounter where Moses did strike the rock, or else they had heard of the episode from those who did witness it. They were probably waiting for Moses to repeat his dramatic action, swinging the staff that parted the Red Sea and hitting the rock once again. When they saw something different, they no doubt would have asked themselves, "What does this mean, that Moses didn't hit the rock but only spoke to it?" *That* was the moment God was waiting for, when the Israelites would be most teachable. But that moment was taken away from God when Moses edited *Speak to the rock* out of the script. God was leading the Israelites to a dramatic, teachable moment and was about to bring the drama to a powerful climax when Moses took the scene into his own hands, making the story about himself instead of honoring the holiness and quiet power of God. He interrupted God's plan and inserted his own lines into the script. And so Moses, who had endured so much for his people, the one to bring God's law to the nation Israel, now forfeited his chance to see the Promised Land with his own eyes.

No—and That's Final!

Just before Joshua was to lead the people into the land of prom-ise, Moses begged God one last time to allow him to join the people and enter the Land. He must have rehearsed this moment for weeks. His pleading worked once before when God was ready to destroy Israel because of all their complaining. At that time, Moses reminded God how forgiving and merciful he was. Moses intervened on their behalf and God forgave them. Surely God would overlook Moses' anger for not speaking to the rock. How could God not cut him a little slack after all the dedication and service he had given God for forty long years, bringing Israel right to the very border of the Promised Land? Apparently, God didn't share Moses' view of break-ing the symbol of striking the rock the second time. Moses pointedly retold the story to the Israelites just before they were to enter the Land. He told them exactly what God said to him.

> At that time I pleaded with the Lord: "O Sovereign Lord, you have begun to show to your servant your greatness and your strong hand. For what god is there in heaven or on earth who can do the deeds and mighty works you do? Let me go over and see the good land beyond the Jordan—that fine hill country and Lebanon." But *because of you* the Lord was angry with me and would not listen to me. "That is enough," the Lord said. "Do not speak to me anymore about this matter."[88]

So Moses was angry due to the complaining of those he was lead-ing. He blamed *them* even though *he* struck the rock. But he had seen God forgive more serious sins in the past and he must have thought right up to the very end that God would forgive him as well, allowing him to join the people he had led for forty years in their victorious entrance into the Land. But that was not to be. When Moses brought

---

[88] Deuteronomy 3:23–26, emphasis mine).

it up one last time, pleading his case with God, not only did God say "No," but he added, *"and don't ask me again."* We've all heard that tone from our parents when we were children. Parents having that reaction are not only angry, but angry and offended that we would even deign to ask. Only when it was time for Moses to die would God let him see the Land, and then, only from a distance, from the top of Mount Nebo,[89] near the Dead Sea. From there, Moses could look over the Land of Promise where the Israelites would meet God's enemies in battle. From there God would show him the only view he was ever going to get in his lifetime. Then Moses would die in bitterness for his failure to obey the command of God to speak to the Rock. This was the Man of God, about whom it would be written: "The Lord would speak to Moses face to face, as a man speaks with his friend"[90] Moses would forever be remembered not only as God's Lawgiver and Friend, but also as the man who symbolically struck the Messiah twice.

---

[89] Deuteronomy 32:48.
[90] Exodus 33:11.

6

Ancient Israel Acting Badly

As you have forsaken me and served foreign gods
in your own land, so now you will serve foreigners in a land not your own.

—God through Jeremiah, Jeremiah 5:19

After leaving Egypt and wandering the desert, the Israelites lived
in the Promised Land just over eight hundred years, from the
time Joshua led the nation into Jericho (about 1400 BC) to the overthrow of Jerusalem by the armies of Babylon in 586 BC. Ancient
Israel existed as a unified nation for almost 500 years before splitting
into the idolatrous northern kingdom of Israel, ruling from Samaria,
and the southern kingdom of Judah with its capital in Jerusalem.
Both northern and southern kingdoms suffered horrific punishment
at God's hand for ignoring and ultimately breaking the covenant they
made with God through the laws given to Moses.[91]

Symbolically, Israel was the wife of God. God laid down the
law, so to speak, but Israel broke God's law by worshiping foreign
gods (symbolically committing adultery with them) and acting badly
in other ways as well. Christians are looking forward to the day when
those in Israel will look on "the one they have pierced" and "mourn
for him as one mourns for an only child."[92] Christians who know

---

[91] Jeremiah 9:13–14; 11:1–5.
[92] Zechariah 12:10.

their Bibles believe this to be Jesus, and they pray for the peace of Jerusalem and of all Israel. Back in biblical days, God sent prophets such as Nathan, Isaiah, Jeremiah, Ezekiel, and others, to warn Israel about the consequences of breaking God's laws. Like actors on a stage, God had Jeremiah and Ezekiel (as well as some other prophets) act out many unusual object lessons over almost fifty years, which got the attention of the people and the leaders of Jerusalem as well as some of the Israelites carried away into exile in Babylon.

The Emotional Impact of Symbolism

Perhaps the most important ingredient of the symbolism in Scripture is the element of strong emotional impact in the listener. Whether it's God urging Abraham to offer his son as a sacrifice, God punishing ancient Israel for sacrificing their children to foreign gods, or God punishing his own innocent Son in place of the guilty, God uses symbolism designed to stir human emotions to demonstrate how he feels about a given situation. These emotions are usually intended to drive us to repent of sins we've committed against God, and then come to him for forgiveness and a loving welcome into his family. The bloodshed of animal sacrifice was meant to demonstrate that sin required a violent death of the substitute that God provided. The symbolism here, clearly, is that God gets very angry over human sin but is willing to accept the sacrifice of an innocent substitute rather than punishing us directly. How much clearer could God be that he loves us and desires to have a loving relationship with us?

Killing the Innocent Lamb

During the first month of the Jewish calendar, on the tenth day of the month, each family in ancient Israel was put on stage to act out a symbolic drama demonstrating the future sacrifice of the sinless Messiah. This Passover feast was instituted just before the Exodus of the Jews from Egypt. Every Jewish family was to select a one-year-old lamb from their flock and care for it until the fifteenth day.[93] For almost a week, that little lamb became part of the family. Imagine the children naming it, playing with it, feeding it, going to sleep with it, only to learn that this new family pet was to be killed and eaten. God wanted the children to learn from an early age that their sins were real and serious. More about the lamb of Passover later.

When David sinned by killing Bathsheba's husband and taking her as his wife, God moved the prophet Nathan to bring to David a symbolic story of David's own sin. Nathan disguised the story to sound like an account of a rich man taking a cute little lamb away from a poor man who had no other possessions. Nathan told David that the rich man served this lamb as dinner to a traveler who had come to him, instead of the rich man taking a lamb from his own flocks. The description of the lamb is very likely how most Jewish families felt about their Passover lambs. Nathan said,

> The poor man had nothing except one little ewe lamb he had bought. He raised it, and it grew up with him and his children. It shared his food, drank from his cup and even slept in his arms. It was like a daughter to him.[94]

God's Symbolic Punishment of David

The injustice of the rich man taking the poor man's lamb and serving it for dinner struck David with such emotional power that he exclaimed, "The man who did this deserves to die!" Only at that point did Nathan say to David, "You are the man!"[95] Of course, David was cut to the heart, understanding immediately the symbolism behind Nathan's story. God punished David for his sins of adul-

---

93 Exodus 12:3, 6.
94 2 Samuel 12:3.
95 2 Samuel 12:7.

tery with Bathsheba and the murder of her husband, Uriah. Again, God spoke through Nathan, saying,

> You struck down Uriah the Hittite with the sword and took his wife to be your own. You killed him with the sword of the Ammonites. Now, therefore, the sword will never depart from your house, because you despised me and took the wife of Uriah the Hittite to be your own.[96]

This shows again how God punishes symbolically: sword for sword. David had Uriah struck down with the sword in battle. Therefore, the sword would never leave David's household. In years following, three of David's sons were violently killed by sword or spear. Amnon by his brother Absalom. Absalom by David's military commander, Joab. And a third son Adonijah, killed on the command of David's son, Solomon, who succeeded David on the throne. The story illustrates how God works symbolically and emotionally in order to get our attention. This helps us understand our sin from God's point of view in a deeply emotional way. (And guess who feels things more emotionally, men or women? More on that later).

Ezekiel and Jeremiah on Stage

Ezekiel began his prophetic ministry in Babylon, where God appeared to him in a vision. He was born into an important priestly family in Jerusalem, the Zadokites (of whom Zadok was a priest faithful to David and Solomon) but was forcibly taken from there while Jerusalem was besieged by the Babylonian army. In Babylon, God had a very important career path in mind for Ezekiel as a kind of actor, where the prophet would act out whatever God told him to do. God even had Ezekiel seemingly make a fool out of himself in order to get across to the Jews in exile the message God had for them. In one instance, Ezekiel had to lie on his left side for 390 days with

---

[96] 2 Samuel 12:9, 10.

very little to eat or drink, representing the 390 years of the northern kingdom's sin against God. Then he had to do the same thing on his right side for 40 days, symbolizing the 40 years of rebellion against God by the southern kingdom of Judah.[97] This must have been quite a conversation piece among the Jews in exile in Babylon.

In Jeremiah's case, he had to be taught about how God thinks before subjecting him to the difficulties that lay ahead of him inside the walls of Jerusalem. When God first called Jeremiah as a boy, Jeremiah complained that he was only a child.[98] And the very first thing God taught him was how to recognize symbolism. God gave him two quick lessons on how Jeremiah would use symbol and metaphor to reach out to God's people. God spoke to him, saying, "What do you see, Jeremiah?"

"I see the branch of an almond tree," Jeremiah replied.

God said, "You have seen correctly, for I am *watching* to see that my word is fulfilled."[99] Although the symbolism is lost in translation, the word *watching* in Hebrew (*sōqēd*) sounds like the word for *almond* (*sāqqēd*). God got a little more calamitous with the second lesson. Again, the Lord said, "What do you see?"

"I see a boiling pot, tilting away from the north," said Jeremiah.

The Lord explained, "'From the north disaster will be poured out on all who live in the land. I am about to summon all the peoples of the northern kingdoms,' declares the LORD."[100] And so began Ezekiel and Jeremiah in their roles as prophets of God, pronouncing judgment upon Judah by interpreting the highly symbolic messages God gave them to act out before a disobedient nation.

Mockers in the Audience

Babylon fought against the Southern Kingdom of Judah and took captives back to Babylon in several stages before finally burn-

---

[97] Ezekiel 4:1–5:12.
[98] Jeremiah 1:7.
[99] Jeremiah 1:11–12.
[100] Jeremiah 1:13-15; When the word LORD is capitalized, the Hebrew word is *YHWH*, also translated as *Jehovah*—the proper name for God.

ing Jerusalem and the temple in 586 BC. Ezekiel, who was taken to Babylon during the second exile, expounded on all the reasons God was removing Judah from the Promised Land. God had Ezekiel "on stage" standing before all the exiles arriving in Babylon from Jerusalem. In one performance with some of the rebellious exiles watching, God told Ezekiel to dig a hole in a wall, then, hiding his face, climb through the wall at night with a bag, packed as if he were trying to escape. Ezekiel did as he was told. The next morning, the people who watched this spectacle the night before asked the predictable question, "What on earth are you doing?" God told Ezekiel how to reply,

> Say to them, "This is what the Sovereign LORD says: This oracle concerns the prince in Jerusalem and the whole house of Israel who are there." Say to them, *"I am a sign to you."* As I have done, so it will be done to them. They will go into exile as captives. The prince among them will put his things on his shoulder at dusk and leave, and a hole will be dug in the wall for him to go through.[101]

Here again, God was trying to shake his people out of their rebellious slumber, using symbols that his prophets acted out. Later, just before the walls of Jerusalem were broken through, that scene literally took place. The prince spoken of in the prophecy was none other than King Zedekiah, chosen by King Nebuchadnezzar of Babylon to rule what was left of Jerusalem after previous attacks on her. Zedekiah rebelled against Babylon, prompting Nebuchadnezzar to lead his army out and attack Jerusalem again. Zedekiah, knowing the end was near, attempted to escape through a gate in the southeast part of the wall during the night. Nebuchadnezzar's men captured him as they fled to the Jordan River valley. They were taken to Nebuchadnezzar, who killed the sons of Zedekiah right in front of

---

[101] Ezekiel 12:10-13 (italics mine)

him and then put out his eyes. As Ezekiel's prophecy predicted, the prince would be captured and *taken* to Babylon, but would *never see it*. He also eventually died there as Ezekiel foretold.

Jeremiah in Jerusalem

While Ezekiel was being used by God among the exiles in Babylon, telling them what was about to happen to Jerusalem, Jeremiah was living in Jerusalem and being used in much the same way among the rebels in Jerusalem.

The Lord pronounced this judgment on Jerusalem through Jeremiah the prophet,

> [Judah and Jerusalem] have returned to the sins of their forefathers, who refused to listen to my words. They have followed other gods to serve them. Both the house of Israel and the house of Judah have broken the covenant I made with their forefathers. Therefore, this is what the LORD says: "I will bring on them a disaster they cannot escape. Although they cry out to me, I will not listen to them."[102]

This covenant demonstrated God's holiness and his protection of Israel's position as God's spokesman to the pagan world around her. In God's mind, this covenant was a marriage covenant between him and his people, Israel. God pleaded with the people of Jerusalem as a husband would to a beloved but unfaithful wife:

> "Return, faithless people," declares the LORD, "*for I am your husband*. I will choose you…and bring you to Zion. Then I will give you shepherds after

---

[102] Jeremiah 11:10-11

my own heart, who will lead you with knowledge and understanding."[103]

Another one of the object lessons God had Jeremiah perform was that of wearing a linen belt. "This is what the LORD said to me: 'Go and buy a linen belt and put it around your waist, but do not let it touch water.'" After Jeremiah bought this belt and wore it, God told him to go and hide it in the rocks. Since Jeremiah was a well-established preacher at this point, people would notice the new belt he wore, and they would notice that one day it was missing. After many days, God told him to go and get it and wear it again. But when Jeremiah dug it up, it was completely ruined. God's message to Judah was this:

> This is what the Lord says: "*In the same way* I will ruin the pride of Judah and the great pride of Jerusalem. These wicked people, who refuse to listen to my words, who follow the stubbornness of their hearts and go after other gods to serve and worship them, will be like this belt—completely useless! For as a belt is bound around a man's waist, so I bound the whole house of Israel and the whole house of Judah to me,' declares the Lord, 'to be my people for my renown and praise and honor. But they have not listened." [104]

God, the Potter of All Nations

Still another important object lesson given to Jeremiah concerned the pot and the potter. Jeremiah was told to go to the potter's house, which he did. The pot which the potter was working on at that moment became marred. So the potter had to change the type of pot he was making. The Lord said to Jeremiah:

---

[103] Jeremiah 3:14-15, emphasis mine. 5:19
[104] Jeremiah 13, emphasis mine.

> Like clay in the hand of the potter, so are you
> in my hand, O house of Israel. If at any time
> I announce that *a nation or kingdom* is to be
> uprooted, torn down and destroyed, and if that
> nation I warned repents of its evil, then I will
> relent and not inflict on it the disaster I had
> planned. And if at another time I announce
> that *a nation or kingdom* is to be built up and
> planted, and if it does evil in my sight and does
> not obey me, then I will reconsider the good I
> had intended to do for it.[105]

This passage is interesting because it doesn't apply only to Israel. It can equally apply to any other nation God raised, including America or any other nation of the West. Of course, the immediate context is certainly Israel and how they had become marred in the hands of God, who is the real Potter, the Creator of nations. But God doesn't limit his blueprint only to Israel. Not only can this passage be *applied* to other nations, in a metaphorical way, but God says *expressly* that this also applies to other nations, whichever way God determines. He says that if he announces a nation is to be destroyed and they repent, God will change his plan and not destroy that nation. You can find a perfect picture of this in the book of Jonah, where God tells Jonah to preach to those living in the Assyrian city of Nineveh that they are about to be destroyed. But the city repents and avoids the destruction planned by God. This clearly demonstrates how God's plans extend to nations other than Israel. The reverse is also true. If a nation is chosen by God to be built up but they do evil in God's sight, he will change his plan for that nation as well and possibly tear it down, which is ultimately what happened to Jerusalem.

---

[105] Jeremiah 18:6–10, emphasis mine.

The West Following in Israel's Footsteps

God gives us one example of a heathen nation—Assyria, marked for destruction, about which he changes his plan. He then gives us the example of his own chosen people, marked for *blessing*, but again changes his plan and sends them instead into foreign captivity (Israel to Assyria, Judah to Babylon). Where, then, do the nations of the West stand? Despite defeats at the hands of Germanic and other tribes (and later by the Muslims) around the Mediterranean in early Christian history, those European tribes were eventually Christianized, and the Muslims were driven out of Europe. There were horrible failures among emperors, Popes, and other Christian leaders through the centuries, killing many who rejected church teaching. But when all is said and done, it was Christian principles that won the day and formed the foundation of emerging European societies. It is clear, given the sweep of history, that God chose the West to be built up as the modern bearers of his message to the world, as proven by the fact that Christianity took root in the West more than in any other region of the world. This is indisputable, despite the many failings of the church along the way, including the Inquisition, the pogroms against the Jews, and the injustices done during the witch trials of Europe and New England. But God raised up the nations of the West due to the growth of the Christian message. God can also destroy them as they walk away from that message.

7

How God Doesn't Think

> I never commanded, nor did it enter my mind,
> that they should do such a detestable thing and
> so make Judah sin.
>
> —God through Jeremiah, Jeremiah 32:35

B efore the overthrow of the houses of Israel and Judah, other nations were sacrificing their children to appease their demonic, pagan gods. Over time, both houses of Israel also started to imitate that practice. The Israelites in the north were supposed to protect the image of God—that deep symbolism where God designed his own nature into each human being. Instead, the northern kingdom fell to Assyria in 722 BC, some two hundred years after forsaking the true God by splitting away from Judah and Jerusalem and following other gods. Even the more godly kingdom of Judah in the south went back and forth, sometimes following God and other times following the wicked nations around them. Eventually, even Judah began sacrificing their own children to the pagan god Molech, burning them alive in ritual fire. Through the prophet Jeremiah, God said,

> The people of Israel and Judah have provoked
> me by all the evil they have done... [T]hough
> I taught them again and again, they would not
> listen or respond to discipline. They set up their
> abominable idols in the house that bears my

Name and defiled it. They built high places for Baal in the Valley of Ben Hinnom to sacrifice their sons and daughters to Molech, though I never commanded, nor did it enter my mind, that they should do such a detestable thing and so make Judah sin.[106]

Molech, which means "king"[107] (similar to the Hebrew *melek*), was the national deity of the Ammonites, who lived just across the Jordan River from Israel and Judah. This might have something to do with God's jealous anger, since the Israelites were *supposed* to be worshiping Jehovah, not Molech, as king. This was an intense spiritual battle where God and Satan were competing for the worship from God's chosen people. Ultimately, Satan won the battle for Israel's devotion. After ignoring many warnings of God's impending judgment, Jeremiah announced God's decision both to the people and to the leaders of Judah: Jerusalem also was to be destroyed, just like the northern kingdom of Israel had been, and Jeremiah would be an eyewitness to that destruction, living in Jerusalem before, during, and after the fall of the city of Great King.[108] God was not about to have his holy name associated in any way with the sacrifice of children by his chosen people.

Symbolic Punishment

Shortly after going to the potter's house, God had another symbolic gesture for Jeremiah to carry out against the southern kingdom of Judah. He told Jeremiah to take a clay pot and lead the elders of Jerusalem to the place called Topheth in the Valley of Ben Hinnom,

---

[106] Jeremiah 32:32–35.

[107] NIV note at Jeremiah 49:1.

[108] "I tell you, Do not swear at all: either by heaven...or by the earth...or by Jerusalem, for it is the city of the Great King" (Jesus, in Matthew 5:34–35).

outside the southeastern wall of the city. This is where child sacrifice had been taking place. There, God spoke through Jeremiah, saying,

> In this place I will ruin the plans of Judah and Jerusalem. I will make them fall by the sword before their enemies, at the hands of those who seek their lives, and I will give their carcasses as food to the birds of the air and the beasts of the earth. I will devastate this city and make it an object of scorn… I will make them *eat the flesh of their sons and daughters, and they will eat one another's flesh* during the stress of the siege imposed on them by the enemies who seek their lives.[109]

The fate decreed to Jerusalem would be devastating. But there is an interesting symbolic angle to this horrible judgment pronounced to the leaders of Israel. God thinks in symbols even when he punishes his own people. While Jeremiah and Israel's elders were standing there at Topheth, the acrid smoke of the last child-sacrifice may still have been hanging in the air, rising from the altar of Molech. In effect, God told them, "I am going to put an end to your child sacrifice because, while the Babylonians are laying siege to your city, there will be nothing to eat inside the city walls. And, you won't be able to come outside the walls here at Topheth to make your horrible sacrifices, or else you will show your enemies a way into the city. Because of the famine, you will be forced to eat your own children rather than sacrifice them in the fire here where we are standing at Topheth. That's how I'm going to put an end to sacrificing your children to Molech, the pagan god and spiritual king of the Ammonites, whom you worship and adore."

In punishing nations (and individuals), God will often design the punishment or trial so that it teaches people how their sin offends him. God instituted animal sacrifice as part of the Mosaic law, but it never

---

[109] Jeremiah 19:7–9, emphasis mine.

entered his mind that his people should sacrifice their own children. That was a corruption devised by God's enemy, Satan, as they were slowly being led astray from their position as God's chosen people. As the Apostle Paul stated in 1 Corinthians 10:20, pagan sacrifices (certainly including child sacrifice) are "offered to demons, not to God."

Again, this breaking of God's covenant with Israel is what prompted God to have them removed from the City of the Great King, Jerusalem. So when difficult or punishing times come—be it to a person or nation—it's important to evaluate whether there is anything in common between that experience and how God thinks about a sin one might be committing. The Jewish leaders would have been wise to understand the symbolism that allowing child sacrifice was just as offensive to God as eating human flesh would be to those leaders. This correlation can be shown like this:

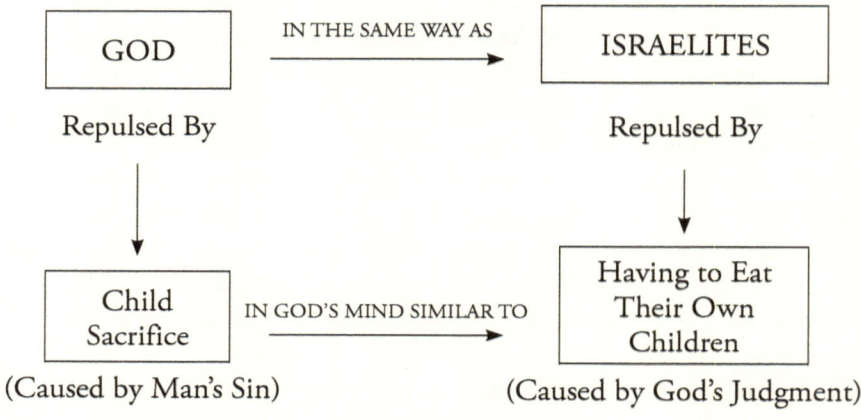

Clearly, God designed a tragic metaphor which would cause the Jews in Jerusalem to be just as horrified and repulsed as God was when they sacrificed their children to Molech. There is a deeply emotional side to God, and Israel was doing things that made him sick. So God devised a punishment that made Israel sick as well. Israel *should* have reasoned, "Hmm, God is doing something that is horrible and repulsive to us. Could it be that we are doing something horrible and repulsive to him?" God doesn't punish randomly, there is always a lesson to be learned from his punishment. And whenever death is the penalty, Satan always stands ready to kill as many as he can. Satan would kill every last person on earth—all made in the image of God—if only God would allow it. Sadly, there was so much calamity in Jerusalem in those days that few, if any, were paying attention to how God felt about anything, and the symbolism was wasted on them.

There at Topheth, after speaking God's judgment to the leaders, God told Jeremiah to "break the jar while those who go with you are watching, and say to them, 'This is what the Lord Almighty says: I will smash this nation and this city just as this potter's jar is smashed and cannot be repaired. They will bury the dead in Topheth until there is no more room."[110] The symbolism of smashing the jar being equal to smashing the city is seen in the words *just as,* which highlight the similarity of the two actions in God's mind. God was in the final stages of allowing Jerusalem to be destroyed and its people transported to Babylon.

The verse at the beginning of the chapter deserves another look because it is God, once again, acting symbolically. The verse reads,

> *As you* have forsaken me and served foreign gods
> in your own land, *so now* you will serve foreigners
> in a land not your own.[111]

God's meaning is plain: if the Israelites refused to serve their God in their own land, but preferred the gods of Babylon, it is only a fitting punishment to allow them to serve those gods in the land where those gods came from. It was a fitting conclusion to ancient Israel's chosen unfaithfulness, and another example of how God thinks symbolically.

Later, in the book of Ezekiel, God gives a similar message of punishment to the nation of Edom. Again, God demonstrated this instructive symbolism in his punishment when he said, "Since you did not hate bloodshed, bloodshed will pursue you" (Ezekiel 35:6).

---

[110] Jeremiah 19:10–11.
[111] Jeremiah 5:19, emphasis mine.

God often shows his displeasure with sinful actions by returning those same actions on the heads of those who do them.

Slaughter of the Innocents

In chapter 16 of his prophecy, Ezekiel recorded these words from God: "You slaughtered my children and sacrificed them to the idols." [112] God considers all children his. They don't just belong to the parents, nor even primarily to the parents. And children certainly do not belong to the government. They belong to God. The leaders of the southern kingdom of Judah had the power to prohibit the sinful activities the people were engaged in but in the end, they let the people have their own way. In fact, there is evidence to suggest that it was the leaders who led the people deeper into sin by their cozying up to the nations around them and to their pagan religious practices. It was King Manasseh who rebuilt the "high places," or places of pagan worship where he sacrificed his own son in the fire of the altar.[113] Manasseh lived only a generation before Jeremiah, and it seems Jeremiah was familiar with what that king and priests of that generation had done. In Jeremiah 32 (referenced above), God placed blame not only on the people, but also on the kings, officials, priests, and prophets of that time. He said, "The people of Israel and Judah have provoked me by all the evil they have done—they, their kings and officials, their priests and prophets, the men of Judah and the people of Jerusalem… They built high places for Baal in the Valley of Ben Hinnom."[114]

By building places of worship for foreign gods, the leaders of Judah were allowing, even encouraging the whole nation of Judah to sin. Although the people themselves desired to worship those gods, it was the leaders who opened the way for the practice to spread like cancer. So, too, the leaders of today's Western nations are, by their laws and judicial opinions, allowing and even encouraging their peo-

---

[112] Ezekiel 16:21.
[113] 2 Chronicles 33:6.
[114] Jeremiah 32:32–35.

ple to sin against God. Who could bring a charge against God if he were to allow his wrath to fall upon us?

Ancient Child Sacrifice and Abortion

There are similarities between ancient times and modern. What's similar is the basic constitution of human and spirit beings. We humans have been made of body and spirit ever since God created Adam and Eve in his image. God and his angels are spirit also.[115] So are Satan and his demons.[116] Since all humans, angels, and demons share this spiritual nature with God,[117] we are all open, to one degree or another, to hearing the words of other spiritual beings. Including evil spirits. And, since we have free will, we humans must all be on guard against Satan's words of temptation. Satan can speak lies into our spirits. If God allows it. In 2 Chronicles 18, a scene from heaven is recorded. God had work to do on earth that required cooperation from a demon spirit. God wanted to lure a wicked king into battle so he would be killed. Yes, God can enlist demons if he so chooses. The demon told God, "I will go and be a lying spirit in the mouths of all his [wicked] prophets."[118] God agreed and told the demon to go and do what he proposed. This is proof that evil spirits can talk directly to, or in this case, through, willing human beings. Those are chilling words.

Just like the ancient nations where Satan was worshipped through offering their babies to Molech, Satan is honored just as much through the more clinical act of abortion, which has claimed more than a billion souls since 1980.[119] When infants are killed in the womb, or worse, born alive and then killed *outside* the womb, there is very little difference between that and placing babies in the molten arms of Molech. Except that the number of babies killed in our day is much higher. How can there not be consequences? Only God knows whether he will eventually punish the West for sacrificing his

---

[115] John 4:24.
[116] Acts 5:3; Luke 11:24.
[117] 1 Corinthians 2:11.
[118] v. 21.
[119] http://www.numberofabortions.com/, retrieved August 21, 2019.

children, just as he punished other nations in the past. But it is pure nonsense to assume his patience will hold out forever. Jeremiah 18, about the potter, demonstrates that the actions of a wicked nation eventually form God's opinion of the entire nation.

Two Groups of Innocents: Any Connection?

We have seen now that God punishes symbolically. Could there, for example, be a possible connection in our own day, between innocent people being shot and killed by mentally disturbed shooters and innocent babies being aborted? Humanly speaking, there is no connection. But could God possibly be saying: "Just as you are taking the lives of innocent babies by a horrible death, I too will allow Satan to take away 'innocent' mothers, fathers and children by a shooter's rampage." Isn't that at least possible from God's point of view? In both cases, the victims are innocent and yet, horrible death is the outcome. But remember—these shooting victims are innocent only from a human perspective. God's assessment from the warnings Jesus gave the crowd in the passages above are that we are all guilty, and if we don't acknowledge Jesus as our Savior from sin, we stand unrepentant before God. Again, Jesus told the crowd to *try hard* to deal with their sins.[120] That goes for us as well. In both cases, the image of God symbolized in man and woman—and life itself—count for nothing. These are the kinds of links we might never find unless we understand how God thinks. If we don't understand why innocent people die at the hand of a shooter, why should we expect God to understand why we abort innocent children? Such a connection may or may not exist, but it is a connection worthy of lifting up to God in prayer. In light of symbolism, this connection makes more and more sense to me. We all need to repent.

At a minimum, idol worship, child sacrifice, and abortion constitute broken symbolism. There are many other examples of broken symbols in Scripture, even going back to the fall of Lucifer, God's most exalted created being and his most trusted protector. This was the beginning of all broken symbolism.

---

[120] Luke 12:58.

8

Lucifer's Metaphor

> Your heart became proud on account of your
> beauty, and you corrupted your wisdom because
> of your splendor. So, I threw you to the earth; I
> made a spectacle of you before kings.

—God's judgment upon Lucifer, Ezekiel 28:17

All the world's a metaphor. How could anything created out of the mind of God *not* reflect his nature in some way or another (unless later marred by sin)? Are we not commanded as part of God's creation to "be holy *because* [God] is holy"?[121] He wants us to be a metaphor of himself. Why? Because God *thinks* in symbols. Living his thoughts after him is how he designed us to live. Even Lucifer, who fell and became Satan, the Adversary, was once a metaphor for the beauty, power, and perhaps even the *justice* of God. But on Judgment Day, he will be judged for corrupting the beauty and power he was created with, thereby symbolically defacing the very image of the God who brought him into existence.

The Making of a Symbol Breaker

Lucifer refused to live in harmony with his Creator. God created him with beauty, power, and authority. Nevertheless, since he

---

121 1 Peter 1:16.

was created as an angel, a member of the elite cherubim to be exact, he was given a nature that would only be completely fulfilled by serving the God who created him. Instead, he believed a lie about himself and his place in God's world. He stole the glory and power God gave him and used it for his own glory—his own personal metaphor—instead of submitting his will and offering back all glory and power to his Creator and Master. There are two relational phrases in Ezekiel 28:17—"on account of" and "because of." These phrases show that Lucifer's beauty and splendor were the cause of two defects in his character: pride and corrupted wisdom. God was not wrong or in any way responsible for Lucifer's downfall just because he created him with amazing qualities.

Lucifer fell because he made a free will choice to elevate himself above his Maker. People can fall just as easily—especially those who have beauty or wealth. Those who have these advantages may have more than they can handle, unless they keep in mind their position before Almighty God. "Friendship with the world is hatred toward God," said Jesus's half brother in James 4:4. In fact, those given greater wealth or beauty in this world actually have a greater responsibility to use it properly before God. Many fail this test. Jesus said, "From everyone who has been given much, much will be demanded; and from the one who has been entrusted with much, much more will be asked" (Luke 12:41b).

Everything about Lucifer's creation was wrapped in symbolism, which, after the Fall, he set out to destroy, seeing how important symbolism was to God. We have seen that, when people corrupt the symbolism behind what God has made, that gets him angry. Satan's objective in our world is to take as many souls away from God and into hell as possible. Each soul he steals is another broken symbol, another insult to the character of God. It is also another soul who failed to understand the symbolism of God and the terrible price to be paid for that lack of knowledge. Since those souls have God's image in them and have eternal existence, Satan may yet have a plan to use those souls as a bargaining chip to lessen his own sentence on Judgment Day. (If you were Satan, wouldn't you try anything you could?) Time will tell.

As far as we know from the Bible, Lucifer was the first created being to rebel against God. This obviously occurred sometime prior to his temptation of Eve in the Garden of Eden. While the record of the Fall is found in Genesis, Lucifer's rebellion occurred sometime earlier on the timeline of history which is not found in Genesis. The only detailed records we have of Satan's first rebellion are shrouded in symbolism in the books of Isaiah and Ezekiel. Each account begins by describing historical human rulers. Then, by expanding the description of these rulers far beyond what any human ruler could possibly attain, the theory is advanced that God was ultimately addressing a super-human power beyond the mere earthly king first described, all of it related in metaphor.

The Rebellion of Lucifer in Isaiah

Isaiah 14 begins with the promise that ancient Judah, after a future exile in Babylon, would once again return to the land of Israel after that exile,[122] and that God would overthrow the King of Babylon because he kept Israel in bondage.[123] Many commentators believe, in a brilliant stroke of metaphor, that these verses have fulfillment in two different characters: the human King of Babylon and the demonic ruler of this world, Satan. But not all agree. Here is the passage from Isaiah 14:3–17, which begins with a prophecy that in the future, Israel will be delivered from the King of Babylon:

> When the LORD gives you [Israel] relief from your
> suffering and anxiety...you will taunt the King
> of Babylon [Israel's captor] with these words:
> Look how the oppressor has met his end!...
> The LORD has broken...the scepter of rulers...
> It angrily ruled over nations,
> oppressing them without restraint...
> Sheol below is stirred up about you,

---

122 See Isaiah 11:11–16.
123 Oswalt, *The Book of Isaiah, Chapters 1–39*, Isaiah 14:1–4.

ready to meet you [the human King of Babylon]
when you arrive…
All of them respond to you, saying:
"You too have become weak like us!…
Your splendor has been brought down to Sheol…
Look how you have fallen from the sky,
O shining one, son of the dawn!…"
You said to yourself, "I will climb up to the sky.
above the stars of El
I will set up my throne.
I will rule on the mountain of assembly…
I will make myself like the Most High!"
But you were brought down to Sheol,
to the remote slopes of the pit."[124]

Here, after God sets Israel free from their coming bondage in Babylon, God instructs Israel to taunt their former captor with those words from Isaiah. Israel is to mock him by imagining the scene in Sheol where the newly killed Babylonian king goes down to meet all the other kings, long dead. They say to him in effect, "You thought you were a hotshot but look at you now. You're not so bad! You're dead, just like the rest of us!" No doubt there is much in this passage referring specifically to the earthly king of Babylon, but some descriptions seem a little too lofty for a human king. For example:

1. The King of Babylon fell from the sky.
2. The king said he would "climb up to the tops of the clouds" and make himself "like the Most High."
3. God calls the king the "shining one, son of the dawn"— quite an exalted, heavenly title for a mere human king.
4. The king said he would set up his throne above the stars of El (which is the Hebrew word for God but could also be used to describe the highest deity among the Canaanite gods).

---

[124] Isaiah 14:3–17, *The NET Bible First Edition.*

Now, these grandiose statements could themselves just be metaphorical, still referring to the human king. But it seems very unlikely that this passage doesn't reflect Satan at all. How could God have missed thinking about Lucifer, the one who tried to defeat Israel at every turn in human history and who probably was the demonic inspiration behind the actions of the King of Babylon in the first place? Satan is ten thousand times more the enemy of Israel than was the King of Babylon. Is it more likely that Satan would watch the demise of Israel from the sidelines, or would he rather take an active role by guiding the earthly king's every move? The Apostle Paul, in Ephesians 6, describes how the battles fought in this world are not physical, but spiritual battles. He says,

> Put on the full armor of God, so that you can take your stand against the devil's schemes. For our struggle is not against flesh and blood, but against the rulers, against the authorities, against the powers of this dark world and against the spiritual forces of evil in the heavenly realms.[125]

Therefore, it seems more likely that the passage deals primarily with the fall of the human King of Babylon. But, in keeping with God's symbolic nature, it also reveals the fall of God's enemy, highlighting the similarities between the pride of the King of Babylon and that of the most rebellious created being of God: Satan—the one empowering, and possibly even indwelling, the King of Babylon and directing his every earthly move.

Who is it who said he will raise his throne above the stars of God? Who said he will make himself like the Most High? It could possibly have been the King of Babylon. That would be the simplest explanation. Or, it could be Satan who boasted of these things. But it is more likely that both are true. If there is any truth in Scripture that such a being as Satan exists, it makes more sense that he actually made these boasts himself but was also speaking through the mouth

---

[125] Ephesians 6:11, 12.

of the King of Babylon. This is an example of "dual fulfillment," used to describe Satan in the heavenly realm, but also describing words spoken by a king in the earthly realm. Dual fulfillment often occurs at two different times—one in the present, and one in the future. In this case, the words were most likely spoken by two persons—Satan, speaking in the distant past—and the king, at the time he ruled Babylon.

Dual Fulfillment in Scripture

The idea of dual fulfillment occurs many times in Scripture, the most obvious being the foreshadowing of the coming Messiah using all kinds of symbolism and metaphor that has both present (to the historical writer) and future fulfillment. Examples of messianic fulfillment include:

- the virgin birth (Isaiah 7:14 and Matthew 1:23)
- the sacrifice of Isaac (Genesis 22:2)
- the tabernacle as a copy of God's temple in heaven (Exodus 25:8–9; Hebrews 8:5)
- water gushing from the rock in the wilderness (Exodus 17:6; Numbers 20:11; 1 Corinthians 10:4)
- manna from heaven (again in the wilderness, Exodus 16:4, 13–15; John 6:31–35)
- the pillars of fire and smoke guiding Israel's journey through the wilderness (Exodus 13:20–22; John 8:12).

And there are many others.

Dual fulfillment and prophecy share the difficulty of keeping separate two events that appear as one. One theologian says of prophecy, "[a]s a picture lacks the dimension of depth, the prophecy often lacks the dimension of time."[126] Again, "all prophecy is complex, i.e.,

---

[126] McClain, "The Greatness of the Kingdom: The Mediatorial Kingdom in Old Testament Prophecy," *Bibliotheca Sacra, 112.*

it sees together what history outrolls as separate."[127] Describing the prior fall of Lucifer in terms of the future fall of another powerful being such as a prince or a king gives readers some clarity and comprehension in symbolic human terms (once the element of time has been added back in) of the horrendous nature of the downfall of a great and powerful metaphysical being.

The Pride of Lucifer in Ezekiel

Lucifer is also described in Ezekiel 28 in another symbolic dual fulfillment. The Prince (or ruler) of Tyre is introduced first (verses 1–10) and is undoubtedly a human character, a proud, human ruler. However, in his pride, he claims, "I am a god [Hebrew *el*]." The local Baal deity was named Melqart, meaning "king of the city" or, more significantly, "king of the underworld."[128] He is also equated with the Greek god Heracles (aka the Roman Hercules). Either the Prince of Tyre was claiming equality with Melqart, or he was claiming equality with the other possible meaning of El, who was the head of the Canaanite pantheon."[129] The pride of the earthly ruler is obvious, but God rebukes the prince saying, "You are a man and not a god, though you think you are as wise as a god" (verse 2). His pride grew as he "amassed gold and silver" in his treasuries due to his skill in trading in the seaside port of Tyre (verses 4–5). In verses 7 through 10, God tells the prince that he is going to die a violent death like a mere man and not like a god.

Then God's narration to Ezekiel switches from the Prince of Tyre to accusations aimed at the *King* of Tyre (verses 11–19). Why the sudden switch from prince to king? This King of Tyre appears to be the demonic force behind the Prince of Tyre. The city of Tyre was (and is) a city on the Mediterranean coast of what is now Lebanon. Beginning in verse 12, this king is described as follows:

---

[127] McClain, op cit, quoting Franz Delitzsch in Herzog's *Real Encyclopedia*, III, 286, quoted by West, *Thousand Years in Both Testaments*, p. 206.

[128] Van Der Toorn, Becking, and Van Der Horst, *Dictionary of Deities and Demons in the Bible*, s.v. "Melqart."

[129] Block, *The Book of Ezekiel, Chapters 25–48.*

You were the model of perfection,
full of wisdom and perfect in beauty.
You were in Eden, the garden of God;
every precious stone adorned you:
ruby, topaz and emerald,
chrysolite, onyx and jasper,
sapphire, turquoise and beryl...
You were anointed as a guardian cherub,
for so I ordained you.
You were on the holy mount of God;
you walked among the fiery stones.
You were blameless in your ways
from the day you were created
till wickedness was found in you.
Your heart became proud
on account of your beauty,
and you corrupted your wisdom
because of your splendor.
So I threw you to the earth;
I made a spectacle of you before kings.

Clearly this description does not describe a mere man, whether a king or otherwise. Again, the most likely scenario is that God is addressing Lucifer, using the human Prince of Tyre as a symbol of another disgraced ruler who was stripped of his power. Lucifer is described as a "model of perfection...perfect in beauty," and as being "in Eden, the garden of God" and "on the holy mount of God." Further, if God threw this king to the earth, we can be pretty sure that this being was originally in heaven with God just prior to being thrown down. No human power could possibly claim this stellar list of accomplishments. The passage must, therefore, refer to Lucifer, who was sworn into service as "the anointed cherub who covers,"[130] or as "the guardian cherub."[131] The Hebrew word for "guardian" is

---

[130] New American Standard Bible, 1995 update.
[131] The Holy Bible: New International Version.

sakak, which has the sense that this angelic cherub was a covering
or protector for God himself, possibly when God was on his throne.
In another sense of the word, Lucifer is seen as "overshadowing"
God, perhaps in more ways than one. There are four other cherubim
described in other places, such as Ezekiel 1 and 10, as the four living
creatures who carry the throne of God from each of its four corners.
They also appear to be protecting the holiness of God.[132] They were
also charged with guarding the way to the Garden of Eden in Genesis
3, so that God's interests there were also protected, as well as protecting man from himself, lest he eat of the Tree of Life and thereby
remain in his sinful condition forever.[133]

Lucifer's Exalted Position

It is possible, therefore, that when he was first created, Lucifer
was the first among five (or more?) cherubim, with four carrying
and protecting the throne of God, and Lucifer perhaps being given
an exalted position above God's throne as one who covers, protects,
stops the approach of sin [from future enemies? unholiness?], and
overshadows the throne of God, to use the various translations of the
Hebrew word *sakak*,[134] or guardian cherub.

The motif of angels guarding the throne from above is not
unknown in Scripture. When God told Moses on Mount Sinai to
build a portable tabernacle for him, God instructed Moses,

> Have them make a sanctuary for me, and I will
> dwell among them. Make this tabernacle and all its
> furnishings *exactly like the pattern I will show you.*[135]

Did you catch the symbolism? Even the wilderness tabernacle
built by Moses was a symbol or representation of God's temple in
heaven. After showing Moses the heavenly temple, the first thing

---

[132] *Bibliotheca Sacra Volume 98*, p.408.
[133] Genesis 3:22–24.
[134] Strong, *Enhanced Strong's Lexicon*, s.v. "sakak."
[135] Exodus 25:8, 9, emphasis mine.

God commanded him to make was the ark of the covenant, the place where God himself would reside. God truly does think symbolically. The ark was to be placed inside the holiest and most restricted place in the tabernacle or, the "holy of holies." This ark consisted of a wooden chest, overlaid with gold, having a lid made of one large piece of pure, hammered gold. Hammered out of the two ends of the lid were to be two angels looking down on the lid from above. This lid of the ark was called the mercy seat and was the actual place where God's presence on earth rested, with two angels (cherubim) overlooking the ark from overhead. Exodus 25:17–22 describes the ark:

> Make an atonement cover of pure gold—two and a half cubits long and a cubit and a half wide. And make two cherubim out of hammered gold at the ends of the cover. Make one cherub on one end and the second cherub on the other… The cherubim are to have their wings spread upward, overshadowing the cover with them. The cherubim are to face each other, looking toward the cover… There, above the cover between the two cherubim… I will meet with you and give you all my commands for the Israelites.

Not only were cherubim designed into the ark of the covenant by God's direction to Moses, but Solomon also designed similar cherubim to hover over the ark in the temple he built in Jerusalem. While Moses' cherubim were smaller but hammered from solid gold, Solomon's cherubim were much larger and carved out of wood then overlaid with gold. These gold-plated cherubim were placed in the most holy place (or "holy of holies"). The room itself measured thirty feet wide and thirty feet long, but the wingspan of the cherubim was also thirty feet, so the angels over the ark completely dominated the room above the ark.

So there is some precedent for having angels hovering above the "throne" in the tabernacle and the temple, just as they must also hover above the throne in heaven. Perhaps Lucifer alone guarded

God's throne, initially, from above. After Lucifer sinned, God apparently placed two other (less powerful) angels there in his place, which became the model for the two replicas placed in the tabernacle and the holy of holies in Solomon's temple. These scenes of heaven are almost beyond comprehension but having Lucifer guard the throne from above is not beyond the realm of possibility. In fact, it would have been spectacular. Lucifer was indeed the most beautiful created being, worthy of ministering in God's presence, and even augmenting (if that were possible) or at least gloriously displaying the beauty of God himself. Merrill Unger described the exalted Lucifer in this way:

> In his pristine sinless state, this mighty angel-protector of the throne of God thus lived in unbroken relationship to the divine holiness... He had access to the very seat of God's authority. He exercised his delegated power in the very heart of God's holy mountain. He guarded the divine throne itself.[136]

If one pictures such a beautiful creature, sometimes walking among the fiery stones and other times as a guardian cherub flying above the throne of God, imagine all the attention he would get as all the other created angels marveled at his beauty and his preferred position among the angels. All that was required was that Lucifer remain cognizant of where his beauty came from, and to remember his place as servant, and God as Master. Instead, Lucifer wanted it all. And because of that, God pronounced, "Your heart became proud on account of your beauty, and you corrupted your wisdom because of your splendor."[137] Lucifer may have thought he was even more beautiful than God himself (despite the fact that all beauty, and everything else, comes from the Creator). As chief guardian to Almighty

---

[136] Unger, "The Old Testament Revelation Concerning Eternity Past," *Bibliotheca Sacra,* 140.

[137] Ezekiel 28:17.

God, the Lord must have given him enormous power—so much that he felt confident he could challenge the God who created him. Due to the glorious beauty and power endowed to him by God, Lucifer became dissatisfied with his appointed position because he was only number two, just behind the Creator of the universe. The result was the casting down of God's highest and most beautiful created being, guaranteeing his eventual judgment and eternal punishment.

Lucifer as Israel's Overseer?

Before Lucifer's rebellion, God may have already had Lucifer pegged for the role of Spiritual Overseer to the future nation of Israel. God foresaw that many people would abuse the free will given to them and would turn away from their Creator and toward created things which they would turn into objects of worship—idols—instead of trusting fully in the Lord their God. This "earth idolatry" worked once before, just before the Flood, and it worked again after the Flood, with the whole world worshipping all kinds of demon deities, bringing all glory to Satan. So God would put his love on one special people to bear his Name amid a sea of unfaithful humanity. It is most interesting to note that God adorned Lucifer with the same precious stones (described in Ezekiel 28) that would one day represent to God's heart all twelve tribes of Israel. The list of stones as given to Lucifer is once again described as follows:

> You were in Eden, the garden of God;
> every precious stone adorned you:
> ruby, topaz and emerald,
> chrysolite, onyx and jasper,
> sapphire, turquoise and beryl.
> Your settings and mountings were made of gold;
> on the day you were created they were prepared.[138]

---

[138] Ezekiel 28:13.

The same precious stones were part of the priestly garment known as the breastplate, worn by Israel's high priest. Compare the list of stones from Ezekiel 28 with the list described in Exodus 28:

> Fashion a breastpiece for making decisions—the work of a skilled craftsman. Make it like the ephod: of gold, and of blue, purple and scarlet yarn, and of finely twisted linen. It is to be square—a span long and a span wide—and folded double. Then mount four rows of precious stones on it. In the first row there shall be a ruby, a topaz and a beryl; in the second row a turquoise, a sapphire and an emerald; in the third row a jacinth, an agate and an amethyst; in the fourth row a chrysolite, an onyx and a jasper. Mount them in gold filigree settings. There are to be twelve stones, one for each of the names of the sons of Israel, each engraved like a seal with the name of one of the twelve tribes.[139]

The stones in the breastplate are all the same, though arranged in a somewhat different order. The one exception is that the precious stones of Israel include three additional stones which are missing from the ones worn by Lucifer. Those are in the third row of the breastplate, including the jacinth, agate, and amethyst. Obviously, at the time God instructed Moses on the making of the breastplate, God well remembered that this list of precious stones he was giving to the High Priest had already been given once before to his number one angel, Lucifer. What could the reason be for this? Perhaps Lucifer was to be not only the overseer and protector of God's throne, but at the same time the overseer and protector of the earthly nation closest to God's heart, which would have needed the most protection from the hostile and demonic nations surrounding them. We know that at this present time, Michael the archangel is the protector of Israel (Daniel

---

[139] Exodus 28:15–21

10:13, 21). Perhaps that role was intended to be given to Lucifer. Whatever the case may be, God was obviously building a symbolic association between the unfallen Lucifer and the nation of Israel by adorning both with an almost identical pattern of precious stones.

One wonders what impact giving the precious stones to Israel's High Priest had on Satan. Though it was perhaps thousands of years after Satan fell, how could he not feel an insatiable hatred toward the weaklings who now had God's favor? The particular hatred that Satan has demonstrated against Israel over the centuries is an indication of the jealousy he harbors against them. If the lists of precious stones tell us anything, they tell us that God thought Lucifer and Israel were very special to God, with Israel being just about three jewels more special.

Next, we will examine the symbolic value of beauty, and why the beauty given to Lucifer was so important to God.

9

Satan's Attack on Beauty and Justice

> In that day the Lord of hosts will be...a diadem of beauty, to the remnant of his people, and a spirit of justice to him who sits in judgment.
>
> —Isaiah 26:5, 6
>
> Your heart became proud on account of your beauty...
>
> So, I threw you to the earth.
>
> —God's Judgment Upon Lucifer, Ezekiel 28:17

In the same way that man and woman were made in God's image, so also were Lucifer's beauty and power a reflection, or image, of those same qualities found in God. And just like Adam and Eve, Lucifer had a responsibility to respect and maintain that reflection of the Being who created him, especially when it came to submitting himself to the will of his Master. Angels and the special order of the Cherubim (of which Lucifer was chief) were created exactly for the purpose of serving God up close. Their importance is seen in Genesis 3 where God placed several cherubim east of Eden to guard the Tree of Knowledge of Good and Evil. Lucifer also symbolized justice since he once hovered above the throne of God, in full and constant view of all other created beings, as a protector of the One who ruled over all creation. But instead of giving God the glory for his own beauty and power, Lucifer chose instead to glorify himself, trying to overthrow the God who made him in the first place. This opened a dark, new world of death or separation from God, as well as opposition to God's beautiful and righteous qualities that would be followed by other unfaithful angels. Since he could not have what he wanted—to be equal with God himself—Lucifer settled instead for receiving his own twisted form of glory from each angel and later, each human being, whom he was able to lure away from God. He exchanged each of his glorious, God-given qualities of beauty, power, and the support and protection of God's justice into their corrupted opposites, like a dark, poisonous cloud seeking to destroy God's best intentions. Satan, at one time second only to God himself in glory and honor, was forced to seek satisfaction from destroying all the symbols that once defined him, including his own beauty. (After all, in Satan's mind, if he could sabotage everything good that God created, wouldn't that also make him equal to, if not greater than, God?) In view of Lucifer's unjust behavior, God removed him from his exalted position above the throne and banished him to the earth. From there, he would set his sights on trashing as much of God's plan for earth and mankind as he could, trading his once-great beauty for ashes.

The Mystery of Beauty

Beauty has a thousand definitions, but one theme is common: Beauty attracts and holds our attention because the beautiful object is so pleasing in the eye of the beholder. But does that really define beauty? Like Truth or Justice, Beauty is in a category all by itself. It is a universal quality with its source and fulfillment in God. One observer tried to put the universality of beauty into words. He said,

> If there is a universal truth about beauty—some concise and elegant concept that encompasses every variety of charm and grace in existence—we do not yet understand enough about nature to articulate it.[140]

---

[140] Jabr, "What is Beauty For?," *New York Times Magazine*, January 12, 2019, 22.

The problem with this observation is that the writer ties the finding of a universal to the observation of nature. This must end in a circular argument because nature consists only in particulars, not universals. If anyone leaves God out of the definition, they will only argue in circles trying to define beauty. The category of beauty is above and beyond all the particular beautiful things one may observe in nature.

Beauty of created things is symbolic of God's beauty and, if we could see him directly, God (being the source of all beauty) would hold our gaze forever. We would never want to take our eyes from him or leave his presence.

Beauty and Justice

Elaine Scarry is a professor of English and American Literature as well as the Walter M. Cabot Professor of Aesthetics and the General Theory of Value at Harvard University. One of her books is an insightful treatise called *On Beauty and Being Just*.[141] There she discusses the characteristics of beauty and our encounters with beautiful things outside ourselves. She may not claim to be a theologian, but she does draw interesting parallels between beauty and justice, two recurrent themes in Scripture and both categories found in God.

She says beauty at first *surprises* us. It welcomes us and holds our attention to the point of making us want to replicate it,[142] whether through painting, taking a photograph, repeating a song or poem, or even through the act of making love, where beautiful new life is replicated from the old and brought into the world. It could be added that, from a Christian point of view, God expresses his own beauty by replicating himself, making man in his own image or by putting his design into each object he creates.

There is danger there, however. Since beauty has the power to hold our attention, God prohibited the children of Israel in the second of the Ten Commandments from making images of things in heaven

---

[141] Scarry, *On Beauty and Being Just*.
[142] Scarry, 4.

or on the earth.[143] If we don't allow beauty to point to the greater category of Goodness, embodied in God alone, we can fixate on or even worship beautiful created things such as angels or demons—widely done by people and nations throughout history. The broken symbol of worshiping other gods was also the chief reason God eventually punished Israel, removing her from her homeland and sending her to Babylon for seventy years. God did make us for worship, among other things, but worship of *created* things was not part of the plan.

Scarry says that when we witness something beautiful, it's as if we have never seen it before.[144] We stare at it and can barely tear ourselves away from it. This explains, at least partly, why God does not show himself to the world in this present age. If he did, everyone would first be transfixed at his beauty—and then *vaporized*, since no one can see his face and live (at least not in this sinful age), according to what God told Moses on Mount Sinai.[145]

Beauty also leads us into a quest for its origin. This is what it means to say that beauty is symbolic of, or *stands for* something else. For Christians and Jews, this "something else" would be God. The power of beauty is attraction. God made human beings to be attracted to the beauty of other human beings. But he also gave us the ability to judge beauty in other parts of creation. God intends that our judgment of beauty will form in us the desire to be in his presence and experience *his* beauty. Scarry puts it this way: "Beauty is sacred."[146] Having once experienced beauty, are we not on the lookout for more of it? When we see beauty in various, different things, we come to the conclusion that beauty is not only in the particular object, but that there is, on a higher plane, a commonality in the very concept of beauty itself. That leads us ever backward in time to the sufficient cause of all beauty, which *must* be God. Scarry says,

> One can see why beauty—by Homer, by Plato, by
> Aquinas, by Dante (and the list would go on...)—

---

[143] Exodus 20:4; Deutoronomy 5:8.
[144] Scarry, 23.
[145] Exodus 33:20.
[146] Scarry, 23.

has been perceived to be bound up with the immortal, for it prompts a search for a precedent, which in turn prompts a search for a still earlier precedent, and the mind keeps tripping backward until it at last reaches something that has no precedent, which may very well be the immortal.[147]

Beauty most certainly does originate with God, the Immortal One, as all who have experienced him know. As David wrote in Psalm 27,

> One thing I ask of the Lord, this is what I seek:
> that I may dwell in the house of the Lord
> all the days of my life,
> to gaze upon the beauty of the Lord
> and to seek him in his temple.[148]

Lucifer's Rejection of Beauty

The beautiful image of God within fallen angels was forever tarnished since they used their God-given free will with their eyes wide open to follow in Lucifer's rebellion. Punishment for them is certain and justified. If the highly symbolic account of Satan's fall in Revelation 12:3, 4 is any indication, then about a third of all the angels in heaven followed in Satan's rebellion:

> Then another sign appeared in heaven: an enormous red dragon with seven heads and ten horns and seven crowns on his heads. His tail swept a third of the stars out of the sky and flung them to the earth.

Lucifer's position was taken away after he rose up against God. Instead of being described as a beautiful cherub, he is now repre-

---

[147] Ibid., 30.
[148] Psalm 27:4.

sented as a dragon. This transformation from beauty to beastly is echoed back in Ezekiel 28. Remember how the ruler of the city of Tyre described himself? He said, "I am a god; I sit on the throne of a god in the heart of the seas."

However, God, speaking through the prophet Ezekiel, corrected the prince and told him, "But you are a man and not a god, though you think you are as wise as a god" (Ezekiel 28:2). Then, as the grandeur of the language increased, the focus shifted to a decree of judgment against both the King of Tyre *and* Lucifer. Recall from verse 17 how Lucifer's beauty and splendor made him proud and corrupted his wisdom. God then took his glory from him and threw him to the earth, making him a spectacle before kings. Verses 18 and 19 continue the thought:

> By your many sins and dishonest trade
> you have desecrated your sanctuaries.
> So I made a fire come out from you,
> and it consumed you,
> and I reduced you to ashes on the ground
> in the sight of all who were watching.
> All the nations who knew you
> are appalled at you;
> you have come to a horrible end
> and will be no more. [149]

As the scene changed from heaven back to earth, the cherub, once filled with beauty and splendor, now an evil spirit being, was thrown out of heaven and seemingly possessed the living body of the earthly King of Tyre, who was mired in sins of his own. According to this interpretation, God apparently continued his punishment to include Satan, who now possessed the earthly king by burning the King of Tyre alive, in full view of a company of watching warriors. The king was reduced to ashes by the fire. But Satan, though not spiritually burned by the physical fire, still got a taste of the destruc-

---

[149] Ezekiel 28:18–19.

tion that would come to him in the future. Satan rejected the beauty and power that was given him, so he no longer represented those qualities of God. His laser light show radiating from his rainbow of gemstones was now replaced with humiliation as the fire burned the earthly king from the inside out, reducing the king to ashes and Satan to some other form of ugliness. Whatever visible state God decided to leave him in, Lucifer certainly lost his claim to beauty. Here, again, is God's final description of Satan and the King of Tyre:

> All the nations who knew you are appalled at
> you; you have come to a horrible end and will be
> no more. (Ezekiel 28:19)

In a stinging rebuke to anyone who forgets God, Asaph, a writer of many of the Psalms, proclaimed that those who rebel against God no longer have any claim to any covenant relationship with Him:

> What right have you to recite my laws
> or take my covenant on your lips?
> You hate my instruction
> and cast my words behind you.[150]

In the same way, Satan lost the right to represent God and so God brought him down in a way that could only be described as horrible.

Two Hearts and Beauty

Beauty is a quality of God, a quality he is well aware of. When given to any created being or thing, it also becomes a symbol of God himself. It might even be said that beauty, like the God who created it, has the power to reveal the thoughts and intents of the heart in one of two ways. Here's how: First, a good heart sees beauty the way God intended for us to see it. We are drawn to it and in some cases seek to

---

[150] Psalm 50:16, 17.

replicate it and even share the experience with others. Having found one occasion of it, we continue the search until we find something of even greater beauty.[151] Ultimately, our search *should* end in our discovery of God, the Author of beauty, but even then, we are still not satisfied until we "have" more and more of God. This is how a good heart experiences beauty.

But there is a selfish way to receive beauty, too, a way which begins with *not* recognizing that beauty has its source in God. If someone captures something beautiful and holds it for him or herself alone, that person first denies that God is the fountain of all beauty and thereby denies God the credit, even the worship that is due to him. Attributing to man (or worse, to the great unknown, or even nature) anything that has God as its origin is a hallmark of humanism or self-worship. This is simple idolatry. Also, that person has kept beauty as well as God, the source of all beauty, from being properly shared by others, interrupting at least one path that could have led others to seek greater beauty that is found in God alone. Beauty is shared among the gracious but garnered by the selfish. What else could be the final end of someone who denies that God is the origin of beauty? Satan is the prime example of such selfishness.

At this point, we should define *humanism* as it is commonly used in this book. We are not using it as a term of general interest in the welfare of people.[152] Nor are we using it to describe the type of Renaissance thinking that was based on the resurgence of classical Greek thought. We are using the following definition:

> The denial of any power or moral value superior to that of humanity; the rejection of religion in favour of a belief in the advancement of humanity by its own efforts.[153]

---

[151] Scarry, 29.
[152] Collins English Dictionary, s.v. "humanism."
[153] Ibid.

The emphasis here is on man's autonomy from God, rejecting God's authority as presented in the Bible and interpreted by the Church through the Holy Spirit, in favor of mankind's definition of meaning starting from his own experience.

Satan's Attack on Justice

As Elaine Scarry points out, beauty has an analogous relationship to justice. Believers would say that Scripture portrays justice as one of God's defining characteristics, and it brings with it an obligation to act justly and to apply justice evenly. Scarry demonstrates how beauty and justice are interdependent. When all things in a society work harmoniously, several principles must be at work. Among them are common values such as strong families, a good work ethic, love, justice, and a defense against the nation's enemies. Freedom of speech and worship should also be present.[154] Throughout time and in all places, there is some form of natural beauty and there are valuable natural resources, making the area a favorable place to live. There might be a beautiful ocean, a lake or mountains, as well as the ever-present beautiful sunrise and sunset, and beautiful stars and other objects or visible events in the night sky. All this beauty in nature is available to people everywhere. But if justice is not operating evenhandedly, then crime will increase and often go unpunished. Order in society begins to break down. Many more are emboldened to break the law. Sin and crime multiply like a cancer.[155] The inevitable outcome is a society that self-destructs. Even after justice has broken down, however, beauty remains evenly displayed among all people, and as Scarry points out when one is lost, the other cries out for its return:

> [Beauty] presses on us to bring its counterpart
> into existence, acts as a lever in the direction of

---

[154] Israel would be an exception to the freedom of religion requirement since God founded that nation to be his exclusively, with punishment for those who abandon him for any other god. The first commandment, "You shall have no other gods before me" bears this out. (Exodus 20:3 NIV).

[155] Ecclesiastes 8:11.

> justice. An analogy is inert and at rest only if both
> terms are present in the world; when one term is
> absent, the other becomes an active conspirator
> for the exile's return.[156]

Justice and beauty also have this in common: They both need protection. When justice breaks down, beauty (or in some cases the loss of beauty) stares people in the face. Lost justice jogs the memory, recalling the former peace and security that once shone like the sun. If some element of beauty remains, according to Scarry, such beauty acts as the seeds of renewal. Slowly, people decide to band together again to protect what is valuable: things like equality under the law, peace, safety, and justice for them and their families. Then, once beauty has been recognized again as valuable and worthy of protecting, it becomes right to protect it, and wrong to destroy it. Since the proper determination of right and wrong behavior are the building blocks of a just society, when a beautiful thing is destroyed, some will rise up in defiance of the destructive act. This defiance is a first step toward justice in those places where justice doesn't already exist or has been badly damaged.

> But when one term ceases to be visible, then the
> analogy ceases to be inert: the term that is pres-
> ent becomes pressing, active, insistent, calling
> out for, directing our attention toward, what is
> absent. I describe this, focusing on touch, as a
> weight or lever, but ancient and medieval philos-
> ophers always referred to it acoustically: beauty
> is a call.[157]

It seems that beauty is an analogy or symbol for justice with both being committed to equality, made that way (in my opinion) by the God who created both. Beauty pushes us toward, and attempts to

---

[156] Scarry, 100.
[157] Scarry, 109, emphasis mine.

guarantee, justice. Only when beauty on earth is utterly snuffed out will justice be unable to return. This explains the schemes of Satan, the "prince of the power of the air,"[158] to advance sin, destruction, death, and eradicate beauty in the world he now rules. What God is implying here is that life is a beautiful gift given to us by God and must be protected. Punishment must be meted out to the offender in order to protect justice. God has made it mankind's responsibility to protect, by the exercise of justice, both beauty and life that God has given them. Without justice, Satan has free reign to "steal and kill and destroy."[159] But one day, the Lord Jesus will return to earth and put Satan down forever, restoring life, beauty, and justice to the earth:

> One of the seven angels…said to me, "Come, I will show you the bride, the wife of the Lamb." And he carried me away in the Spirit to a mountain great and high, and showed me the Holy City, Jerusalem, coming down out of heaven from God. It shone with the glory of God, and its brilliance was like that of a very precious jewel… The foundations of the city walls were decorated with every kind of precious stone… The great street of the city was of pure gold, like transparent glass… Nothing impure will ever enter it, nor will anyone who does what is shameful or deceitful, but only those whose names are written in the Lamb's book of life… No longer will there be any curse.[160]

What a beautiful sight that will be!

---

[158] Ephesians 2:2 (ESV).
[159] John 10:10.
[160] Revelation 21:9–11, 19, 26; 22:3.

10

Gender Symbolism in Adam and Eve

Adam named his wife Eve, because she would become the mother of all the living.

—Moses, Genesis 3:20

Some have said women are the weaker sex. As I saw him, my dad was very strong during the war—at least according to his commendations and medals. But my mother was stronger in other ways—especially in areas that mattered to me most—like keeping me alive. That took a different kind of strength. For my father, PTSD led to alcoholism. That affliction burdened him for the rest of his life. My mom never seemed to focus on herself very much. She was always looking out for my brother and me. Our lives depended on it. I never thought my mom was weak.

The Account of Creation from Genesis 1

When God created Adam, he purposely created him to be weak. Yes, he was strong enough to tend the Garden and do all the tasks required to subdue the earth. He was marginally stronger than Eve and stronger than many of the animals. But he was weaker than God because that's how God designed him. There was never any delusion in the back of Adam's mind that someday, he would be equal to God. The psalmist wrote,

You made him a little lower than the heavenly
beings [161] and crowned him with glory and honor.

God also had a lot of experience with *strong* created beings. God
gave Lucifer strength and beauty at the time of his creation. His glory
exceeded that of all the other angels, archangels, seraphim, and cherubim. Lucifer was second in power only to God himself, but Lucifer
became proud and fell from his exalted position. This created the
father of all headaches—for God, and the rest of creation. God certainly didn't want a repeat of that situation by loading up Adam with
knowledge and power during his first day on the job. Better to lay
it on him slowly, and let him understand with every new lesson that
God was always going to be *Numero Uno*. These lessons would also
have to be shared with his wife, once she came on the scene. But up
to this point, Adam didn't even know he was going to *have* a wife. Or,
for that matter, what a wife was.

Though Adam and Eve were both created on day six of creation, they were not created at the same moment. This was made
clear by Moses giving the Creation account *twice*, once in the first
chapter of Genesis and again in chapter 2, with a different emphasis
and different details given in each account. Before God created Eve,
God needed to teach Adam a little about the garden. There was danger within and without. Adam wasn't stupid. Once Eve was created,
he realized he was bigger and stronger than she was. He would be
responsible for keeping his wife and children safe from the evil that
lurked in the garden. The first lesson was: Don't eat from the tree
over there, in the middle. Adam also had to name all the animals
before Eve was created. Naming the animals could have taken quite a
while, depending on how many animals he had to identify. I suspect
it took just long enough for Adam to realize he was lonely.

God's purpose in recounting the Creation story in Genesis 2
was to fill in some of the details regarding Adam's need for a helper
who hadn't been created yet. Even with the new details of Genesis 2,

---

[161] Psalm 8:5,6; Hebrew for "heavenly beings" is *Elohim,* Septuagint: *angels.*

questions remain. What *is* clear is that a fair amount of time elapsed between the creation of Adam and the creation of Eve.

God Reflected in Adam Reflected in Eve

Genesis 1 records the creation of man like this: "So God created man in his own image, in the image of God he created him, male and female he created them."[162] Since a sign is something that stands for something else, God made Adam and Eve to stand for, or represent, God himself. The fact that Adam was made in God's image makes it crystal clear that Adam was a symbol of God. Then God created Eve, also in God's image. But since she was taken from Adam's rib, she was also made in the image of Adam.[163] So the woman embodied two images, making her a symbol of God and a symbol of Adam.

God thinks symbolically. What he creates from his mind also contains deep, wonderful symbolism reflecting his character. When God declared he "saw all that he had made, and it was very good,"[164] he meant it. And he was pleased with his creation of Eve. (I'm sure Adam wasn't too upset either). When God looked at the relationship between Adam and Eve, he saw his own relationship with those believers who would one day place their faith in him—Adam representing God and Eve representing all believers, joined together in a loving marriage covenant. God didn't just create Eve to bring life to the world, have fun, and have Adam around for comic relief. God

---

[162] Genesis 1:27.

[163] And yes, while Adam may have had one less rib than Eve, his DNA was likely unchanged, providing future generations of males with the original twelve pairs of ribs, the same number as their female counterparts.

[164] Genesis 1:31.

had a much bigger design in mind. This symbolism can be represented like this:

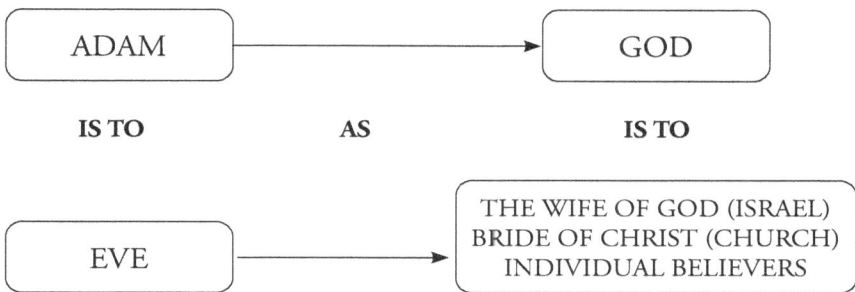

Genesis 3:20 says, "Adam named his wife Eve, because she would become the mother of all the living." Since Eve is the mother of all human beings (except Adam), she became a kind of matriarchal head of all human beings. When Adam saw Eve, he saw her through human eyes, as a wife, a companion, a mother. But what did God see when he looked at her? He saw all those things and more. He saw all human beings through her—all those to whom she had given life— but especially those believers redeemed by the Messiah from Israel and the Church, since those believers all stand in a marriage covenant with God—he being their spiritual husband and they his wife.

The Symbolism behind Eve

If God had wished to create a partner for Adam who was equal to him in every way, then God could easily have made a twin brother from the same dirt Adam was made of, and given both of them a supernatural formula to create an army of additional baby boys out of the ground. Then God would have many equal partners, neither one weaker than nor very different from the other. But that wasn't God's plan. God wanted to devise a way to demonstrate his deep longing and desire to interact with his new human creation. He wanted to show human beings, though they were *weaker* than God, that they could still have a meaningful relationship with God. A relationship in which they would *want* to submit to God's loving leadership. This relationship would show God for who he is: a strong, powerful, yet loving and caring God.

How to Design a Metaphor

Suppose you were God, and you wanted to design a metaphor that represented your loving relationship to Adam, the pinnacle of your creation. Suppose, further, that you didn't want the metaphor to overtly refer to yourself, thereby giving away the meaning. How would you do that?

This metaphor would explain how much you love Adam and want him to voluntarily commit to a binding relationship with you. This has to be a metaphor that people through the centuries would *want* to participate in, just as much as you (God) want them to join in a covenant of love with you. Keep in mind that, as God, you want to highlight your own faithful love and commitment to each new human being. If they got into trouble, you would rescue them, show them forgiveness, and continue loving them. You would want the metaphor to demonstrate how humans could rely on you and trust you to protect them after seeing how strong you were, even though there were strong enemy forces allied against you.

What metaphor would you create? Perhaps you might create just one human being, Adam, having only one gender and the ability to self-propagate. This creature might express love and obedience at first, but, over time, life might get a little boring. What would guarantee he wouldn't tire of being your servant and pursue his own interests and express his own freedom? Adam would have little reason to love and worship you. Instead, he would join together with another man and form a metaphor where Adam was equal to you. You've already seen that movie, when you created Lucifer as your near equal.

Or you might create an android, programmed to be devoted to you. But would love that didn't come from free will bring you any satisfaction? Or you might create one human and maybe a pet for him to love and train. The pet might love you and follow you around, but the pet would have limited intelligence. No self-respecting human being would want to be part of a metaphor where one of the participants was equal to a pet. Not even God's pet. That would be insulting.

No, you're trying to create an earthly relationship that simulates your love for your creation, but without telling them that's what they're simulating. How about creating two, three or four genders and create their human natures in such a way such that they interact in a loving way. (Something like that seems to be going on in our day). But if they were equal in strength, there would be constant tension between them. Petty jealousies would also be sure to arise, so that probably wouldn't work either.

This is the metaphor God decided on: the beautiful *Eve*.

Explaining the Metaphor

God created two new creatures, one slightly different from and physically a little stronger than the other. He would be called Adam, or Man, and would be the leader, just as God is the leader. The one who was just slightly weaker (physically) would be created from the man and be called Eve, or Woman. In exchange for a little less physical strength, God gave Eve a stronger emotional nature, allowing her to feel and understand the human condition much more deeply than the man. He also gave her more beauty. God and marketing experts know this to be true, given the share of beauty products, hair styles, clothing, perfume, and jewelry devoted to the female market. Eve would also be given a very strong love and desire toward her husband. But most of all, she would be the source of all future human life. She would be alive in ways that far exceeded her dull and boring husband. Now, the stronger one would symbolize God—not that God is dull and boring. This man would be unsatisfied until he found his mate. God would design the man with a strong desire to seek out a mate, because God is always in the process of seeking out lovers from among all human beings. Once the man and woman found each other, they would be joined together in spirit and share their love with each other, hopefully forever—though Satan already had designs for breaking these unions apart. This bond of love would still demonstrate the kind of relationship that God desired from each human being. God would prove his love to that new creature by one day visiting them in human form and dying to save them from the Enemy. He also wanted to display how he hoped each person would respond to his love. As the Apostle John said in just three words: *God is love.*[165]

God would love and cherish his new creatures in a greater (but similar) way that Adam would love, honor, and cherish his new bride. Eve would respond to her husband with her own love and bring new life into the relationship.

Rejecting the Metaphor

That is exactly how God designed the human metaphor. The sad thing is, the further our culture gets from its Judeo-Christian roots, the less marriage looks like the metaphor God created it to be. Satan has done much to destroy it, even in recent times. Laws making divorce difficult to obtain have been dissolved and courts have ruled against traditional marriage, legitimizing every form of sexual perversion.

My own story is that I, too, had wrong ideas when I entered into marriage. Though becoming a Christian several years before, I didn't yet grasp the metaphor that I should treat my wife as Christ loved the Church. Nor did my parents have a good marriage that I could model my own after. It took time to learn that as the husband, faithful love toward my wife was my chief responsibility, as God faithfully loved me. But that knowledge came too late to save my first marriage.

Many women have been told since childhood that they are weaker than boys or men. They have taken this physical weakness to mean that they are weaker in every sense. This translates into "women are worth less than men." It has given some women cause to reject the metaphor as God designed it. But *worthless* is not how God views women. And it should not be, must not be, how boys and men view women. The gentle feminine nature was designed by God because God himself has that same nature. God sees women as beautiful, desirable, and deserving of special treatment, including love and romance from their husbands. In order for the symbolism

---

[165] 1 John 4:8.

to work God simply *had* to make the female slightly weaker than the male. But he made them much more beautiful and desirable. Peter described the kind of beauty God desires most in a woman:

> Your beauty should not come from outward adornment, such as braided hair and the wearing of gold jewelry and fine clothes. Instead, it should be that of your inner self, the unfading beauty of a gentle and quiet spirit, which is of great worth in God's sight.[166]

In a very real sense, a woman's outward beauty is symbolic and a reflection of a woman's inner beauty. The very reason God made Eve slightly weaker, but also gentler, more emotional, and more beautiful than Adam was because those were exactly the characteristics that God saw in *all mankind,* both male and female. Not only is God attracted to those qualities in human beings, but a man also sees those feminine qualities of love, beauty, and a more delicate nature as greatly attractive in a woman—they are the very reason he is attracted to her in the first place. When a man understands the gentler nature of a woman, he is closer to understanding his own relationship to God. It's all part of the metaphor. Therefore, no man who mistreats his wife has any real understanding of God.

Sin has spoiled our understanding and broken the symbolism behind male and female. But in the salvation achieved by the sacrifice of Jesus, God begins a spiritual rebuilding process in each person who commits him or herself "in marriage" to God. God begins to restore our insight even before we see him face to face. He created us to be a desirable and loving partner to worship and adore him forever and ever, even though we are weaker than he is. "As a bridegroom rejoices over his bride, so will your God rejoice over you" (Isaiah 62:5b).

In marriage, God's desire is that man and woman exist in a loving relationship that exemplifies God's love for his people. Both should strive for love and respect toward one another, keeping intact the spiritual symbolism found in human marriage.

---

[166] 1 Peter 3:3–4.

11

Creation Symbolism Broken

> You are free to eat from any tree in the garden;
> but you must not eat from the tree of the knowl-
> edge of good and evil, for when you eat of it you
> will surely die.
>
> —God to Adam, Genesis 2:16–17

> And you must not touch it, or you will die.
>
> —Eve to Satan, Genesis 3:3

God created all things for his good pleasure: the earth, the seas, the animals, and man and woman, to whom he gave dominion over the earth and everything in it. Everything God created was symbolic of what was in his mind, an expression of his good and loving nature, a nature he wanted to share with billions of human beings. Adam and Eve were created to represent God and humanity, respectively. They were to protect the symbolism within them by obeying the commands of God, as he taught them, little by little, how to fulfill their purpose in the world. "They will all be taught by God"[167] was the Maker's credo for all mankind, and so some knowledge was necessarily withheld from Adam and Eve until the proper time.

---

[167] Isaiah 54:13; John 6:45.

The Tree of the Knowledge of Good and Evil was one such prohibition. The tree that was forbidden to Adam was exclusively God's domain for the time being. The very fact God was willing to put it "in the midst of the Garden" tells us that God wanted it to be a sort of focal point for Adam and Eve as they tended the garden—something for them to respect, ponder, and one day achieve mastery over.

Trouble in Paradise

For God, the Tree of Knowledge was more than just a tree. He infused its physical fruit with the metaphysical knowledge of good and evil. To this day, a tall, sturdy tree symbolizes wisdom and knowledge. Allowing Adam and Eve to walk near that tree spoke of the kind of close, trusting relationship God was willing to have with them. It should have inspired the obedience he expected from them. Over time, they would gain wisdom through their stewardship of the garden, and one day God would share the knowledge of good and evil with Adam and Eve as well—but not before they were mature enough to handle that knowledge with the caution and restraint that it deserved. Unfortunately, the day for learning about evil would come too soon.

Somehow, Adam failed in his responsibility to make his case to Eve that the Lord's command regarding the Tree of the Knowledge of Good and Evil was to be fully and unquestionably obeyed. Knowledge of evil was in its fruit, a poison that could burn through human history like a fire through a dry forest, turning God's creatures against him. The fact that knowledge of evil was part of the tree's fruit shows that Lucifer's rebellion had already taken place and evil had begun its reign throughout the angelic realm in heaven. God in his wisdom had kept that knowledge from Adam and Eve thus far and they would be safe so long as they obeyed God's command not to eat of the Tree. This is not altogether different from parents protecting their children from the knowledge of certain evils until they are better prepared to understand them. Even today, are there not things like the atrocities of war that can traumatize even the most mature adult? A lot must have been at stake, including keeping the "image of God symbolism" unbroken within them, thereby upholding the holiness of God in the face of his enemies.

What's on the Menu?

Eve had not yet been created when God gave Adam authority over the Garden of Eden, so she missed the initial instruction that the fruit of the Tree of Knowledge must not be eaten. However, she was present when God told them both that they could eat from every seed-bearing plant and from *every* tree having fruit with seeds in it.[168] Eve said later that this fruit was "good for food." So even the fruit of the Tree of Life must have had seeds in it. But God made this tree an exception to the rule. Still, Adam should have clarified to Eve that God gave him an additional command stating that the tree in the middle of the garden, though "good for food" was still off-limits and that she would die if she ate from it. In any event, Eve relayed her understanding of God's command by saying to the serpent,

> You must not eat fruit from the tree that is in the
> middle of the garden, *and you must not touch it,*
> or you will die. (Genesis 3:3, emphasis mine)

What is often missed about Eve's declaration is this: What she told the serpent simply *wasn't true*, and Satan zeroed in on the mistake. Where did Eve get the and *you must not touch it* part of the command, allegedly spoken by God? Was Adam afraid Eve wouldn't take the prohibition seriously and so added that last part to the command himself? Did Adam say something like, "Eve, just to be safe, let's not even *touch* the tree, or else we might die?" Or did Eve simply want to add her own thoughts to what Adam told her regarding God's warning? Whatever the reason, since either Adam or Eve (or both) misquoted God, that inaccuracy awarded to the serpent *game, set, and match.* Here's how.

---

[168] Genesis 1:29.

Satan, Evil Genius

Eve handed Satan a logical, and unassailable reason to question God's command, since it was now mixed with error. To understand this point, we need to look briefly at the rules of logic and how Satan took advantage of an error made by, or at least repeated by, Eve. Consider the following two phrases, coupled with the word *and*:

> Human beings need oxygen to survive,
> AND
> the moon is made of green cheese.

There are rules of logic (a branch of philosophy) that determine whether this whole statement is *logically* true or false. Since the two phrases are connected by the word *and*, the whole statement is true *only if both phrases are true*. The first phrase is true but, since the second phrase is false, the whole statement becomes false because using the word *and* tightly couples the two phrases together. Each phrase no longer stands on its own. But if we changed the word *and* to *or*, that would change things quite a bit. Consider this example: If the rulers of Athens told Socrates, "You must drink orange juice *and* hemlock," then the old philosopher would certainly die. But if they gave him this choice, "You must drink orange juice *or* hemlock," then Socrates could have had a nice glass of OJ on the rocks, then continue agitating the local authorities.

When Eve discussed eating the fruit with Satan—her first mistake—she answered Satan in a way that made God's command untrue and Satan took advantage of her error. "Oh, come on, that's ridiculous!" you might say. But if you're a genius like Satan, and you see an error in logic, you'll jump all over it because you *know* the statement is now false. And that's what Satan did.

Now, look again at what Eve said and how Satan responded. Eve told Satan she was not allowed to eat from the tree, *and* she couldn't touch it or she would die. Satan jumped on the second part of the statement—"you must not touch it"—and because that part was false (since God never said it), Satan could say with authority,

"You will not surely die." [169] With one of the two phrases now false, Satan could legitimately cast doubt on what Eve *thought* God commanded. That left God saying one thing, Satan saying another, and Eve with the tie-breaking vote. Her desire for the fruit overruled her desire to obey Adam, so she took it and ate it. This shows what a master deceiver Satan was (and still is). As Paul later said,

> For Adam was formed first, then Eve. And Adam
> was not the one deceived; it was the woman who
> was deceived and became a sinner.[170]

If Eve was deceived, what was Adam's excuse? The only thing worse than walking into sin with one's eyes clouded with uncertainty, is walking into sin with eyes wide open. Both of them should have rebuffed Satan by quoting God's actual words. When the Lord Jesus was tempted by Satan in the wilderness (in Luke 4), he answered each temptation with God's exact words from Scripture. That was enough to make Satan back down. Eve at least made an attempt to quote God's command back to the serpent, but Adam made no effort at all. He simply ate the fruit when she gave it to him. No doubt he would have walked off a cliff as well if she had asked him.

Eve's error should be a warning to us all that Satan will exploit any error in our belief and twist it into a path toward sin any time he can. This becomes a victory for Satan and a further claim on our lives when Satan accuses us before the throne of God. By the way, men are not immune from Satan's deceit either, but in this case, Eve was the target. If anyone had any doubt about the conniving brilliance of God's once-greatest creation, you may now lay aside your doubt. Because of Satan's mastery of twisted logic and deception, he has many more followers on earth than God does. Truly, narrow is the road that leads to life, and sadly, only a few find it.[171]

---

[169] Genesis 3:4.
[170] 1 Timothy 2:13, 14.
[171] Matthew 7:14.

Eve 2.0

One can, perhaps, draw additional conclusions about what Adam and Eve were thinking at the time of the Fall by looking at the different "punishments" God gave to each after they had sinned. Rather than punishments, these pronouncements were more like new boundary conditions. They were not, however, *curses* that God laid upon Adam and Eve, as is sometimes believed. Genesis 1:28 says, "God blessed [Adam and Eve] and said to them, 'Be fruitful and increase in number.'" God doesn't curse what he has already blessed. We see proof of this in the story of Noah, where Noah got drunk and two of his three sons walked into Noah's bedroom backward with a garment to cover his nakedness.[172] The third son, Ham, *looked* on his father's nakedness (and, according to the Hebrew, may have done worse than that). What did Noah do in response to Ham's actions? Did he curse Ham? No, because God just finished *blessing* Noah, Shem, Ham and Japheth in Genesis 9:1. So Noah cursed Ham's son, *Canaan*, instead.

In the Garden, God didn't curse Adam or Eve, but he did give each of them a new measure of physical discipline. It wouldn't make any sense for God to leave Adam and Eve in the same condition of freedom they were in when they sinned. Without some kind of constraint added to their human condition, the whole creation could just spiral out of control and the entire enterprise would be lost to Satan. To make it a little harder for Adam and Eve to sin, God cursed *the ground* that Adam would have to cultivate, making it physically more painful for him to live. More discipline would be required on Adam's part to provide the basics needed to live his life. However, God did curse the serpent who started the whole thing, saying,

> Because you have done this,
>   Cursed are you above all the livestock and
> all the wild animals!

---

172 Genesis 9:20ff.

You will crawl on your belly and you will eat
dust all the days of your life.[173]

Pain can humble the strongest will. Therefore, God added a
new dimension of physical difficulty for Adam to struggle with, to
keep him out of trouble. God did the same to Eve. To her, God
declared: "I will greatly increase your pains in childbearing; with pain
you will give birth to children."[174] What was intended to be a joyous
experience—that of bringing new life into the world—would forever
be marked with pain. Women would now be kept humble through
both menstrual pain and the agony of childbirth. All that was a new
physical hardship, not unlike what God added to Adam's condition.

In addition, God made a "metaphysical" change to Eve. *Meta* in
Greek means "after" or "beyond." Aristotle coined the term when he
needed a title for the volume that came after his *Physics*, so he named
it *Metaphysics*, or *After Physics*. Genius! But "metaphysical" has also
come to refer to the knowledge that describes what comes after or
beyond the physical being, such as the intangible soul or spirit of a
being. When God first created Eve, he not only copied the *imago Dei,*
or image of God from Adam into Eve, but God also took a greater
measure of Adam's emotional nature and gave it to the woman. Eve,
ever since she was created, had a slightly stronger emotional makeup
than what God left within Adam.

A Woman's Heart, according to the Research

This difference would not have been lost on Satan. He observed
this difference and chose Eve as his mark rather than Adam. The
difference in Eve's thinking would forever be guided *slightly* more by
emotion than by her more rational side. Obviously, emotions play
a role in decisions made by men *and* women, but women generally seem to feel emotions more deeply than their male counterparts.
According to one researcher, women are more likely than men to act

---

[173] Genesis 3:14–15.
[174] Genesis 3:16a.

with empathy and in ways that minimize suffering.[175] For example, women reacted more negatively to unpleasant slides (e.g., mutilated bodies, physical violence, and suffering or dead animals), a sex difference that persisted in size from ages 20 to 81.[176]

Other researchers found that women react with significantly more sadness to sad films than men do.[177] Sometimes this is good, sometimes not, but it just might be that females are more like God, not less, emotionally speaking, than males. In Scripture, God in the Old Testament and Jesus in the New are often portrayed as feeling more deeply about suffering than the often less-emotional average male. When Jesus wept at the tomb of Lazarus, it was not recorded that any of the other disciples wept as well.[178] In the book of Jonah, God told Jonah to warn the people of Nineveh that their city would be overturned in forty days.[179] When God saw that the people repented, he withdrew his threat to destroy them, making Jonah angry. God confronted Jonah about his attitude. He said to Jonah,

> Nineveh has more than a hundred and twenty
> thousand people who cannot tell their right hand
> from their left, and many cattle as well. Should I
> not be concerned about that great city?"[180]

Jonah wanted judgment but God used this change of plan to demonstrate his *compassion* toward people and animals. God is both just and compassionate. It seems he demonstrated both sides of his character in creating Adam and Eve, Adam having a greater mind for judgment and Eve a greater mind for love and compassion.

Here's the tricky thing about human emotion: Emotion is never wrong. After all, how can it be wrong to *feel* something? After Satan

---

[175] Schmitt, "Are Women More Emotional Than Men?" *Psychology Today*, April 10, 2015.
[176] Schmitt, citing Gomez, Gunten, and Danuser.
[177] Schmitt, citing Kring and Gordon.
[178] John 11:35.
[179] Jonah 3:4.
[180] Jonah 4:11.

countermanded God's command not to eat the fruit, Eve debated what to do next. That was her second mistake. She knew it was wrong but gave in to her feelings instead of resisting them. She felt it would be okay, since the fruit looked good to eat, and was "desirable for gaining wisdom."

After the Fall, God found it necessary to address this emotional part of Eve's spirit, not in a harsh way, but in a loving way that has benefitted men and women through the ages. Since Eve acted independently of Adam before her disobedience in the Garden, God made a change to Eve's spiritual programming—a metaphysical change to her soul and spirit. God told her, "Your desire will be for your husband, and he will rule over you" (Genesis 3:16b). By saying "*will be*," God was making it plain that she was not *previously* acting according to her desire for, or obedience to, Adam. Going forward, Eve, by feeling an even stronger desire or love for Adam after the Fall, would be less inclined to act independently of his desires. For untold centuries, love has been described as a "pain" or a "weakness" by men and women alike, but the woman's deeper and more emotional love for her husband is evidence of this metaphysical change that God placed within the married woman's spirit.

This change to Eve's spirit might have simply been an enlightenment of sorts. The forbidden tree contained not just knowledge of evil but also of good, knowledge to which they previously had no access. God's word is so powerful that when God spoke his correction to Eve, the information he imparted to her, previously hidden, now shined a light of understanding into her spirit, awakened by the marital commitment to her husband. He might have given her and all married females from that point forward, new insight into the meaning of love—*your desire will be for your husband*—and her symbolic nature as one of support and help to her husband—*he will rule over you*.[181] It's also possible that, before the Fall, Eve was less emotional and afterward, God may have slightly increased her emotional sensibilities. I'm not saying God gave her Love Potion Number 9,

---

[181] Genesis 3:16.

where Eve started kissing everything in sight.[182] But a slightly deeper emotional nature would also result in a deeper love for Adam. With these changes, Eve and her daughters would forever be a light and life for their husbands much in the same way that Wisdom is personified as a female in the book of Proverbs. With her enhanced emotions, Eve would be a voice of wisdom to her husband to give emotional support and strength to his position of family leadership.

Regardless of the nature of the change made to Eve, this condition imposed by God upon women has been cursed by feminists throughout the ages, yet they are powerless to fight against it. God has metaphysically transformed the desire in a woman's heart from an independent free-spirit prior to marriage, to a human spirit that is less independent and more loving toward her husband after marriage. This spiritual change within Eve allows (even causes) her will to be directed toward, and, to some degree molded, around the will of her husband, all in the name of love. It would not be an exaggeration to say that directing Eve's love in such a way that *her desire will be toward her husband* is one of the greatest gifts that God has ever given to the human race, especially to men. It also urges the husband to treat his wife with additional love and respect because of her new position with regard to her husband, just as God has greater love for those who have committed themselves in "marriage" to God. As St. Peter told his readers,

> Husbands, in the same way be considerate as you
> live with your wives and treat them with respect
> as the weaker partner and as heirs with you of the
> gracious gift of life, so that nothing will hinder
> your prayers.[183]

By the way—this spiritual change within Eve parallels the experience of someone who is without God for part of his or her life, but then receives Jesus as their Savior and begins to live their life to

---

[182] Song lyrics by Jerry Leiber and Mike Stoller, 1959.
[183] 1 Peter 3:7.

please God. There, too, God makes a spiritual change within that person, allowing them to desire God in ways they never would have otherwise known. There are many such parallels within marriage that relate to one's receiving Jesus as Savior and Lord.

The Wrath of the Feminists

Now, of course, feminists would deny this truth to their dying breath about the wife willingly submitting to her husband. Most would deny that any metaphysical change occurs to a woman's mind after marriage. Early feminist Charlotte Perkins Gilman wrote back in 1898, "There is no female mind. The brain is not an organ of sex [i.e., gender]. [You might] as well speak of a female liver."[184] It is true there is no difference between a male or female liver and the evidence is also gaining strength that there is no difference in the anatomy of male and female brains as well (other than their size), but the female *spirit* which takes residence, or at least operates, *in the brain is* different, in ways we have only begun to explore. By equating mind with brain, Charlotte Perkins was wrong. There may not be a female brain, but there *is* a female mind, simply because there *is* a female spirit. As mentioned before, God created the woman, soul and body, from the part removed from Adam. If there were no female spirit, feminists would be at a loss to explain *any* metaphysical differences between men and women, and it is often the case that feminists do deny that such differences exist. (*Soul* and *spirit* are often used interchangeably in the Bible, comprised of mind, will, and emotions).

To deny the spiritual differences between Adam or Eve would be to completely ignore not only the mounting empirical evidence,[185] but also the symbolism designed by God into male and female genders. It would also mischaracterize God's sovereign, loving intentions for his new creatures. For Eve, God's most beautiful creature, an independent will *left intact* which ignored gentle but firm warnings against danger would have been the bigger punishment, one that

---

[184] Gilman, Women and Economics, 74.
[185] See Schmitt.

would have made the woman's relationship to both God and man much more adversarial.

Adam 2.0

For Adam's part, God imposed upon him a new condition of anguish through resistance to his working of the soil. Now, through weeds, pests, diseases, and adverse weather conditions affecting the planting, maintenance and harvesting of crops, Adam's working of the soil would become much more burdensome. Occupying more of Adam's free time with work is what God had in mind, which would later birth a new proverb: "Idle hands are the Devil's workshop."[186] His normal existence *prior* to the Fall probably was a lot more lei- surely and successful as he worked the soil. He worked at a more leisurely pace. Maybe a little gardening in the morning followed by long coffee breaks and trying to impress the new lady friend in the afternoon and into the evening? (Do you *really* think things were *that much* different back then? Replenishing the earth takes time!) It's not a stretch to imagine that Adam was torn between wanting to please God and wanting to please his new flame. But with the earth no lon- ger yielding its crops quite so easily, much more time would have to be spent at work and not at play.

---

[186] Attributed variously to St. Jerome or Chaucer (in the *Tale of Melibee*).

12

New Testament Marriage Symbolism

> This is a profound mystery—but I am talking
> about Christ and the church.
>
> —Apostle Paul, Ephesians 5:32

I t is not just the Old Testament that emphasizes the symbolism
found in the microcosm of marriage. In Ephesians 5, Paul lays
out various responsibilities of the man and the woman in a marriage,
then he pulls a fast one and gives one of the most startling examples
of marital symbolism in the New Testament. By changing the focus
from the human sphere to the heavenly sphere, Paul provides all the
proof necessary to confirm the symbolic nature of gender and its
understanding within marriage.

Marriage as a Microcosm

Paul discusses, as he often does, how Christians should live in
order to please God. They should please God because they are made
in the *image* of God, and doing his will is a human responsibility.
Paul lists many good and wholesome points which a Christian will
follow if they are living by God's Spirit and by his power. These are
not "laws" to be obeyed grudgingly, as if God is trying to keep us from
living a fun life. Rather, the Christian life, lived through the power of
the Spirit, will lead to a loving, peaceful, fruitful, and deeply mean-

ingful existence. Those who live this way will receive God's blessing. Among the guidelines in Ephesians 5 are these:

- Verse 1: Be imitators of God (since we carry God's symbolic image).
- Verse 2: Live a life of love.
- Verse 3: There should be no hint of sexual immorality, impurity, or greed.
- Verse 4: No obscenity, foolish talk, or coarse joking
- Verse 8: Live as children of light (in goodness, righteousness, and truth).
- Verse 11: Expose "deeds of darkness" done by others.
- Verse 20: Be thankful to God the Father for everything.

These rules to live by summarize what it means to live as a being made in the image of God. Violating any of these rules breaks the image-of-God symbolism with which man and woman were created.

Paul continues with a few other instructions, then launches into some *dos* and *don'ts* that apply to authority structures involving Christians. These include the submission of one Christian to another, slave to master, child to parent, and yes, wife to husband. These rules are not mastered by self-effort, but by living according to the power of the Holy Spirit.[187] Paul begins with a simple command to all Christians: "Submit to one another out of reverence for Christ."[188]

For those who are single, this should be the norm, since they do not fall within the authority structure of marriage, other than their symbolic (but very real) union with Christ. The Lord Jesus modeled this notion of submission or servanthood throughout his ministry, that whoever wants to be greatest must be servant of all.[189] He himself came to serve, not to be served.[190]

---

[187] Galatians 5:13–16: "Serve one another in love. The entire law is summed up in a single command: 'Love your neighbor as yourself.' So I say, live by the Spirit."

[188] Ephesians 5:21.

[189] Matthew 20:26–27.

[190] Ibid., v. 28.

Submission in Marriage

After laying down this general principle of submitting one to another, Paul then applies it to the marriage covenant. He begins with wives, stating that they should submit to their husbands just as they do to Jesus himself. As we have seen, there is deep symbolism here which is the reason behind the command. The symbolism is this: "For the husband is the head of the wife as Christ is the head of the church, his body, of which he is the Savior."[191]

Here is that symbolism in diagram form:

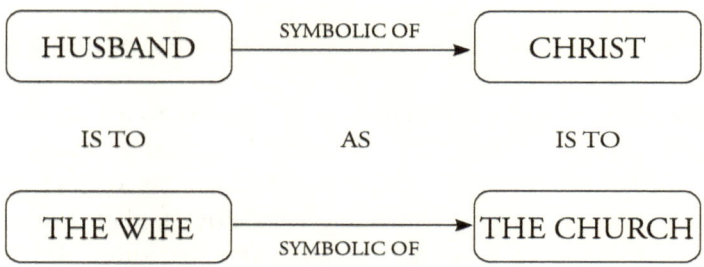

Simply put, the husband is symbolic of Christ and the wife is symbolic of the entire church. After Paul's comments to wives, he exhorted each husband to love his wife in the same way that Christ loved the Church. That's a pretty high bar. In essence, the husband shouldn't ask his wife to do anything that is in any way sinful (on the negative side) and requires men to always and proactively treat their wives in a loving (even romantic) way. Just as evil is aggressive in this world, so also Jesus' love was and is aggressive to those within the family of believers, and even to those outside it. Jesus is the model for a husband's love toward his wife.

It has been noted by some teachers that Paul is reminding each spouse to do what *does not come naturally* to that spouse. If Paul had asked the wife to love her husband, that wouldn't have been too great a challenge since wives are naturally given to loving not

---

[191] Ephesians 5:23.

just their husbands, but showing love and compassion toward just about everybody. (That's the norm but, naturally, there are exceptions). However, for a wife (who can take care of *herself*, thank you very much), *submitting to her husband* is rather more a challenge. Submitting to her husband is to recognize and respect the *position* that God has placed him in as head of the family, even though he may or may not deserve it (depending on the day of the week). Again, respect for the symbolism that lies behind marriage *is how God thinks*. God expects that the symbolism behind marriage not be broken. This is a foreign concept to the modern mindset. Therefore, one has to choose which mindset one wants to obey—the mindset of God or the mindset of Satan, who tries to lure human beings into violating every boundary and break every symbol God has placed within Creation. Those are the only two options.

With so many women in the workforce, the importance of the husband showing love to his wife is all the more important. With wives sharing the stress of holding down a job outside the home, it goes without saying that she will have times where she will need the help of her husband to do some of the tasks inside the home which she otherwise would gladly have done herself. The husband will be the one submitting to her in cases like this. So submission is part of love and works both ways.

One thing many women seldom get enough of in marriage, though they may not ask for it, is *romance*. After a woman has submitted herself all day to a tough manager, or tough children, the last thing she needs is to submit to an authoritarian husband. Men would do well to learn more how to please their wives romantically, which is different from pleasing them sexually. With men and women living to please each other in marriage, what need would there be to look for romance outside marriage? Romantic love is expressed beautifully in the Song of Solomon. And if the man is symbolic of God, then the primary lesson from the Song should be that God romances us with his love, and delights in doing so. God does this in order to get us to respond to his love so that we may truly be one with him as a husband is one with his wife. The Shulamite in the Song responds amazingly with her love and devotion to Solomon. When he feels her love, no doubt he feels like he owns all the gold in the world—which Solomon nearly did.

Paul used the Christ-and-Church metaphor to show how important it was for husband and wife to fulfill the roles they were created for. Clearly, God represents the completely *faithful* husband to his Church, the Bride of Christ, spoken of symbolically by the Apostle John in Revelation 19:6–8:

> Hallelujah!
>
> For our Lord God Almighty reigns. Let us rejoice and be glad and give him glory! For the wedding of the Lamb has come, and his bride has made herself ready.

If God uses marriage symbolism about us to tell us how much he loves us (despite our sinfulness), then we really don't have much excuse to not show the same love to our spouse.

Ending Ephesians 5 with a Shocker

Paul ends the section on husbands and wives in Ephesians 5 with a shocking statement about marriage. After going through all the details of love and respect between husband and wife, Paul closed that discussion by saying he wasn't even *talking about* marriage.

> "For this reason a man will leave his father and mother and be united to his wife, and the two will become one flesh." This is a profound mystery— but I am talking about Christ and the church.

First, Paul quotes Genesis 2:24 that describes the three principles of *human* marriage. Then he turns around and says in effect, this has never been said before, but God was talking about *Christ and the Church* way back in Genesis! Marriage was just the symbol of Paul's real concern, that being the covenant relationship between

God and the believer. Of course, the principles in Ephesians 5 apply to the symbol of marriage as well, but Paul certainly gets our attention by reminding us that God's relationship to us is what really counts. Marriage is just the symbol of that relationship, and it's up to us not to break that symbol. The relationships of husband and wife, and Christ and the Church are so close, that they are practically interchangeable.

God made human marriage to *fully* represent the covenant God has with those who love him. In order not to break that symbolism, the man must unconditionally love his wife like God loves us, and the wife must submit to her loving husband just like individual believers are supposed to submit to God. And neither one should be hard to do when you're in love. This completely fulfills the definition of a sign or a symbol: One thing is set up to "stand for" something else. What a beautiful symbol God has set up to represent Christ and the Church! Paul sets the bar pretty high, but love flows deep when symbolism is fulfilled.

Marriage Symbolism Means Intimacy with God

We think in symbols and God thinks in symbols. So What? Well, try this: God made us think a lot like he does so we can actually get to know him a lot more personally, even intimately, than most people realize. In fact, God wants to teach us many things about himself and develop a *romantic* relationship with us, à la Song of Solomon. God flat-out *wants* a love relationship with every human being because "God is love."[192] But to reach this level of intimacy means that both God and man (or woman) must become vulnerable to one another, just as in any human romantic relationship. If we live in close communion with the Holy Spirit, God allows us to draw very close to him. But as for outsiders, those who live for self and care nothing about God, those he keeps at a distance, never fully understanding God or having much of a relationship with him.

---

[192] 1 John 4:16.

Bride for Isaac, Bride for God

In another brilliant display of symbolism, God gave us the story of how a bride was obtained for Abraham's son, Isaac.[193] It doesn't take much imagination to figure out what God wanted to portray to mankind in this story: Abraham represents God the Father. Isaac represents God the Son. And Abraham's servant represents the Holy Spirit. Abraham told his servant to go and find a bride for his son Isaac. So in symbolism, God the Father sent the Holy Spirit to find a bride for the Lord Jesus, the Son of God. And that is exactly God's primary focus since the beginning of human history. The Holy Spirit is, even now, actively seeking a bride for God the Father, those who want a deeper love relationship with God. As the Lord Jesus said, "A time is coming and has now come when the true worshipers will worship the Father in spirit and truth, for they are the kind of worshipers the Father seeks."[194] Human beings who willingly worship God in spirit and truth are the "brides" of God, whether they are Jews under the Old Covenant (where they were known as the wife of Jehovah[195]) or as the bride of Christ in the New Testament.[196] Understanding this role of God and his bride is deeply symbolic. Making sure you are part of his bride by worshiping in spirit and truth is the most important responsibility that God has entrusted to each person.

Learning How God Feels

Getting married is an eye-opener for both husband and wife, but continuing to struggle through the difficulties every marriage brings will help each spouse see an aspect of how God loves individuals in the Church. Participating in that symbolism helps each person submit to the other and to show patience and forgiveness to one another. If we come to see that human marriage requires love and submission, it will be easier to understand a relationship with God. If

---

[193] Genesis 24.
[194] John 4:23.
[195] Jeremiah 2:2; 3:14, 20; Hosea 2:2, 19; Isaiah 54:5, 62:5.
[196] John 3:29; 2 Corinthians 11:2; Revelation 19:7.

we reflect on the difficulties that loving a spouse presents us with, it is easy to see that we ourselves also bring heart-wrenching difficulty to God on occasion. As noted earlier, women seem to feel emotional pain more deeply than men do. That is very likely due to the fact that God gave greater emotional depth to the woman than he did to the man. God himself feels very deeply the pain caused by sin as the Lord Jesus demonstrated with weeping over the death of Lazarus in John 11, or when he grieved over Jerusalem in Luke 13:34, where he longed to gather her children to himself, but they were not willing. Even so, God remains committed to us and continues to love and forgive us. Putting ourselves in God's sandals (and understanding how he always forgives us) can help us forgive others more readily and can make us more cognizant of ways we sometimes hurt the Lord. As we receive more insight and apply the symbolism behind marriage to our own lives and actions, we will grow in love toward our spouses and toward God. By maintaining the symbolic roles God created in marriage, we live in accord with creation and with God's plan for humanity—that is, to live in unbroken symbolism with our Creator on earth, preparing all of us for a husband-wife relationship with God for all eternity, where all of us are the weaker partner and God is forever the strong and loving husband.

Walking Toward the Light

Even if a husband or wife doesn't believe in God or what marriage stands for, the power of marriage symbolism can still function as guardrails for the people involved. God can use the lessons each one learns in marriage regarding love, submission, respect, and keeping vows, to keep them more or less aligned with the truth that God demonstrates in his covenant with the individual believer. In this way, a married couple, even though not yet believers, can take steps toward the light and renounce the darkness, which may open their minds to additional teachings from God, and possibly even to a saving faith if they continue in the grace that comes by obeying the symbolism created through the act of marriage. A person can't be saved by obedience to marriage alone, or by obedience to any of the signs God has established, because a person who tries to live obediently to God's symbolic principles (such as marriage) is still a sinner in need of the substitutionary work of the Lord Jesus as payment for their sins.

Still, an unbelieving married couple who stay faithful to each other is in a better place to have a relationship with God than, say, a married couple living in a sexually "open" relationship. The traditional couple, though not yet Christians, still understand some of God's important principles found in marriage, whereas the second couple has stepped outside the symbolism God intended for marriage and broken that symbolism, especially in the area of sexual fidelity. It only stands to reason that God may find it easier to draw nonbelievers to himself if they don't *hate* what he stands for—that is, if they don't hate his symbolism as expressed in marriage.

Likewise, when a nation renounces age-old principles regarding one-man-one-woman-forever marriage, that nation is placing itself at great risk of losing some of the grace that God previously poured out on them. The salvation of many souls is ultimately at stake when God's symbolism is "cleansed" out of a society.

Breaking Marriage Covenant Symbolism

The God who created the universe wants a love relationship with each human being. This is beyond amazing. From the human perspective this means learning to love God and learning not to trample on his character as represented by the symbolism he has revealed in Scripture. To continue to trample the various symbols that God has instituted will mean eventual judgment and certain death, followed by eternal separation from God and from those who love him with an undying love.[197]

Isn't it obvious, then, why (except in the case of sexual sin) a man should not divorce his wife? Considering the symbolism behind divorce, this would represent God changing his mind and breaking off his love and covenant with us, his bride. And if a woman

---

[197] Ephesians 6:24.

divorces her husband, it symbolizes a believer casting off his or her faith in God, deeming God as somehow unworthy of our dedication and love. That broken symbolism is a slander and a defamation of God's character, and Satan is always there to take full advantage. Regardless of whether there are legitimate charges against a partner on the human level, the symbolism is still broken. With this in mind, Jesus's unflinching commitment to the marriage covenant is better understood. Can anyone fault the Son of God for adhering to the permanence of marriage as God originally conceived it?

Jesus spoke to certain Pharisees, the most learned men regarding the Scriptures, about the permanence of marriage as God designed it. Here's the story:

> [The Pharisees] asked, "Is it lawful for a man to divorce his wife for any and every reason?"
>
> "Haven't you read," he replied, "For this reason a man will leave his father and mother and be united to his wife, and the two will become one flesh?... Moses permitted you to divorce your wives because your hearts were hard. But it was not this way from the beginning. I tell you that anyone who divorces his wife, except for marital unfaithfulness, and marries another woman commits adultery... The one who can accept this should accept it."[198]

How much more obvious does God need to be before we begin to understand how important symbolism is to our Heavenly Father? Remember that God *thinks* in symbols, and so should we.

What the Lord Jesus gives us here is practically a definition of what a broken symbol is: a hardness of the human heart when it comes to understanding the symbolism behind an act of God. Jesus understands that our marital pain tolerance is less than optimal because our

---

[198] Matthew 19:3–12.

hearts are hardened with sin. But he correctly defends the symbolism involved with marriage and divorce and ends his thought with this encouragement: "The one who can accept this should accept it." It is better not to separate what God has joined together. But Jesus also understood there would be those who would not or could not accept his teaching. For those circumstances where a breakup is unavoidable, people have the freedom to choose divorce. However, divorce, like all broken symbolism, often carries its own punishment.

13

Sexual Symbolism

The body is not meant for sexual immorality but
for the Lord, and the Lord for the body.

—Apostle Paul, 1 Corinthians 6:13

When God designed human sexuality, he had several symbols
in mind. God *did not,* however, summon all his creative powers merely to provide pleasure on demand for hungry hedonists who
care nothing for God or his purposes for mankind. With Satan's help,
this is what God's second greatest gift to the world has devolved into.
(Second only to salvation from death through Jesus). Perversion and
broken symbolism were certainly not the objectives God had in mind
when he created the ecstasy of the human sexual experience. God
intended this, like all the rest of his creation, to be symbolic, thereby
bringing himself glory when the symbolism behind the experience is
observed and triggering punishment when it is not. The symbolism
God intended is fulfilled every time a husband and wife express their
love to each other and confirm their faithfulness to the marital covenant. He also created man and woman to have an ecstatic, *spiritual*
covenant relationship with God and the sexual act is the perfect way
God chose to demonstrate it. It was not made for those outside marriage to carry out their sexual fantasies or perversions. God's blessings
toward mankind were not meant to exist in fleeting, non-binding
relationships.

Today's Hedonism

Hedonism is a good way to describe the increasingly popular attitude toward sexual freedom in today's western culture. Hedonism is the philosophical theory of ethics "in which pleasure is regarded as the chief good or the proper end" of human activity.[199] There are several varieties of hedonism, depending on whether the hedonist is after his own pleasure, or the pleasure of society as a whole. There are also other factors involved in defining hedonism. You have to take into account what counts as pleasure and whether that pleasure is short-term or long-term. At one time, you also had to consider whether your reputation would suffer, or if any consequences would soon follow.[200] But in today's world, at least among non-believers, consequences and reputation seem to be of little importance. At least until Judgment Day.

For Procreation Only?

Despite having encased proper sexual behavior in civil law in ancient Israel, making it a model for all future civilizations, God also designed sexual intercourse for the promotion of oneness in marriage, the propagation of the human race, and even for enjoyment between husband and wife. Many Bible expositors believe Catholic theologians got it wrong when they said that intercourse is primarily for procreative purposes. That idea goes at least as far back as Augustine in the 4th century. In his *Against the Manicheans*, Augustine wrote,

> In marriage, as the marriage law declares, the man and woman come together for the procreation of children... Where there is a wife there must be marriage. But there is no marriage where

---

[199] Compact Edition of the *Oxford English Dictionary*, "hedonism."
[200] Gosling, "hedonism," *The Oxford Guide to Philosophy*.

motherhood is not in view; therefore neither is there a wife.[201]

The Bible never teaches that motherhood must be "in view" for there to be a valid marriage. The truth is that God defines a marriage by three principles and only three:

1. Man must leave father and mother.
2. Man must be joined (read that as "committed") to his wife.
3. The two shall become one flesh.

If children are given to them by God along the way, all well and good. But if not, there is no cause to think any less of the marriage much less, to terminate it. All three steps point to one common element: *commitment.* Following those three steps fulfills the requirements of marriage symbolism in God's eyes when he joins a couple together, and that union should never be broken, because God himself has joined them together (Matthew 19:6). Other steps can be added to God's marriage pact (such as a lavish ceremony, certification from the state, and medical tests), but nothing can be taken away from those three essential elements.

By the way, here's a clue for the men: Genesis 2:24 in another translation reads, "man shall leave his father and his mother and *hold fast* to his wife."[202] The Hebrew word for "hold fast" has the sense of to "follow hard," "overtake," or "pursue closely."[203] Ever hear of the expression, *women like to be pursued?* This is sometimes expressed, usually in a non-verbal manner, at the start of a relationship. When Moses wrote those verses in Genesis, he was certainly familiar with human nature and the game of pursuing a marriage partner. This is another mystical element of marriage symbolism that God has built into the human image of God.

---

[201] St. Augustine, Against the Manichæans; Morals of the Manichæans; ch. XVIII.65.

[202] Genesis 2:24, ESV.

[203] Strong, *Enhanced Strong's Lexicon*, Woodside Bible Fellowship, Heb. "dawbak."

God always intended that sexual relations *only* be engaged in as part of a committed marriage relationship. The reason why is deeply rooted in symbolism. First of all, in the same way that the man pursues a woman who has stolen his heart—the story that launched a thousand songs—so God is the one who first pursues a relationship with a man or woman (or even a child). Rarely, if ever, is the one being sought truly interested in God when he begins to show interest in them. If the person responds to God's calling (God, in the person of the Holy Spirit), by receiving Jesus Christ as their Lord and Savior from sin, they are, in effect, accepting an offer of marriage from God and his promise of commitment. From that point forward, their sins are forgiven forever and God's commitment to them can never be broken. As seen in the chapter on marriage, this is why human marriages should also remain unbroken. A broken marriage implies that God's love for his bride is somehow imperfect and therefore doesn't last forever or else the bride becomes disinterested in God or finds some fault in him. Both scenarios are impossible in our relationship to God. His love toward us is utterly unfailing and our pleasure from being in his presence will never be exhausted. Of course, there is complete forgiveness for the many who have broken the symbolism behind marriage, but God continues to hold the standard high and desires that the metaphor of marriage be respected, at least by whomever is able to accept this difficult teaching.[204]

Sexual Symbolism and Spiritual Knowledge

In biblical times, the verb *to know* was sometimes used in a sexual context. For example, Mary used the term in questioning the angel Gabriel during the discussion of Mary's Immaculate Conception by the Holy Spirit. As Luke related the story, God sent Gabriel to Mary in Nazareth. Gabriel's words would rock this teenager's world forever:

> Do not be afraid, Mary, you have found favor
> with God. You will be with child and give birth

---

[204] Matthew 19.

to a son, and you are to give him the name Jesus.
He will be great and will be called the Son of the
Most High.[205]

Mary's fear was understandable. First, she was a teenager about
to become pregnant, with a son who already had a name. This son
was the promised Messiah, the Son of the Most High—that would
be God. So God was his Father, and that would make Mary the
wife of God, and mother of the Eternal King, right? That's a lot to
swallow for a teenager, if she could even put it together that fast. It's
amazing she didn't pass out right then and there. She didn't show an
ounce of disbelief, never asked for a sign, and didn't put God or angel
to the test. There was never a doubt as to the veracity of the angel's
testimony. However, Mary *did* ask Gabriel, "How will this be, since
I am a virgin?"[206] The original Greek wording of that phrase is "how
will this be since I have never *known* a man?" (literally, "*since man I
know not*").[207] This demonstrates the use of *knowledge* in a sexual way.
Her bewilderment was justified, but nothing is impossible with God.
Gabriel told her, "the Holy Spirit will come upon you, and the power
of the Most High will overshadow you."[208] Mary would *know* when
her conception was taking place because she would have a very close
encounter with the Holy Spirit. While there was no oneness of flesh
as in a human marriage, there definitely was a oneness of God's Spirit
with her spirit. It was not *carnal* knowledge, but it certainly was a
deep and wonderful spiritual knowledge.

This language—*the Most High will overshadow you*—feels very
offensive to many who subscribe to feminist ideologies. The idea that
a man, or God or anyone else would take a superior position, "overshadowing" a woman—especially in a sexual context—demonstrates
to a feminist how women continue to be sexually oppressed through
possession and domination.[209] According to some feminists, no one

[205] Luke 2:30–32.
[206] Luke 1:34.
[207] Nestle-Aland Greek New Testament, Greek "ginosko."
[208] Luke 1:35.
[209] Dworkin, *Intercourse*, 79.

should be overshadowing anyone else or else there will be oppression. Andrea Dworkin (1946–2005) expressed her revulsion this way:

> [Intercourse] is taken to be her capitulation to him as a conqueror; it is a physical surrender of herself to him; he occupies and rules her, expresses his elemental dominance over her, by his possession of her in the [intercourse].[210]

Mary, in the view of the radical feminist, must have been oppressed by God in the same way. Feminist author, Sarah McDavitt Woods, in her hate-filled article, *Jesus was a Rape Baby*, also echoed the opinion that Mary, mother of Jesus, was overshadowed by God, making him a rapist and predator. She wrote:

> Mary was not a "wild child" but a girl living in a rigid patriarchal world who was raped by her husband, a soldier, or some other predator. In the Biblical narrative, that predator was God. God the Father "overshadowed" the child bride Mary, impregnating her with his one and only son, the reported savior of the world.[211]

In marriage, the idea of sexual or carnal knowledge is highly symbolic of God's knowledge of a human spirit when God joins his Spirit to the spirit of the believer. And yes, this act of knowing is indeed a sort of spiritual "penetration." God makes no apology for that—it's all wrapped up in the term *knowing*. There is an interaction between God and a human being where he penetrates the soul of the willing believer, which God likens to the pleasurable experience of a man knowing his wife sexually. This is the most intimate symbolism in the Bible, all made possible by God's creation of the marriage metaphor. This knowledge in our relationship with God works both

---

[210] Ibid., 79.
[211] Woods, "Jesus was a Rape Baby," *Medium*, retrieved February 28, 2018.

ways. In the same way that both spouses gain intimate knowledge of each other when they become one flesh, so God *and* the believer gain deep, intimate knowledge of one another when they commit themselves to each other, spirit to Spirit.

That human beings gain intimate knowledge of God is made clear in 1 Samuel 2. In that story, the priest named Eli had two wicked sons. The narrator says that these men did not "know" the Lord.[212] This is our same word used for carnal knowledge elsewhere in the Bible, including in 1 Samuel 1:19 where it says, "And Elkanah *knew* Hannah his wife, and the LORD remembered her [i.e., the Lord allowed her to get pregnant whereas before she was barren.]" The two sons were wicked because they *did not know* the Lord, as was expected of all believers. The word for intimate knowledge was used in both contexts. One was physical knowledge and the other was spiritual knowledge, used to describe our relationship with God.

It is difficult to conceive that our coming to know Christ as our Savior brings deep pleasure to God, but it does. Every human being who has ever lived has the power to withhold his or her affections from God. The Holy Spirit is constantly searching every heart to see whether there is any fertile ground on which to plant a seed that might lead to a desire to know God. Naturally, Satan also has the power to take that seed out of someone's heart.[213] God derives great satisfaction from bringing life to a barren heart. Sexual satisfaction on the human level is proof of how God feels about our coming to "know" him as our Savior and his coming to "know" us on an intimate level as well.

We've noted how God designed human romance to parallel the spiritual feelings God wants between himself and those who love and worship him. There are other parallels in human courtship as well. As previously discussed, the male in a marriage is the representation of God who is the husband to the church (or to Israel, take your pick of metaphor) which in turn is represented by the female in a human marriage.

---

[212] Hebrew "yaw-dáh," to know; Strong, *Enhanced Strong's Lexicon.*
[213] Matthew 13:19.

God: Passive or Aggressive?

To push the symbolism a little further, who would you say in real life is generally more sexually aggressive—the male or the female? And who *was* slightly more passive, modest or inhibited—again, generally speaking (and *before* they started handing out condoms in public schools)? The very natures of male and female are symbolic to God. This is not true in *all* cases, but in human relationships, the male was always seen as more aggressive while the woman was almost always a little more passive or at least cautious (until Christian virtues were thrown to the wind in the 1960s). God designed this to be the case. The symbolism is this: Because of sin, all humanity (represented in God's mind by the female) is disinterested in God. If God didn't send his Spirit to come and woo or draw many back to himself, *no one* would have come to God of their own volition. We humans, in the God-human relationship, are quite resistant to God, who is very interested in becoming our husband. In Romans 3, the Apostle Paul quotes Psalm 14 and Psalm 53 (which are virtually identical to each other—perhaps for emphasis). They read in part:

> There is no one righteous, not even one;
> there is no one who understands,
> *no one who seeks God.*

Perhaps this is why God gets so excited when people join themselves in a love-covenant with him. He is the one who initiates the initial contact with us but as we know, "many are invited but few are chosen."[214]

The Feminists' Attack on Marital Symbolism

Now we press sexual symbolism to the max. The act of sexual intercourse is itself deeply symbolic to God and may be the second most important symbol that God ever devised (after Jesus as the

---

[214] Matthew 22:14.

Sacrifice Lamb). This arrangement of the male lovingly penetrating the female sexually in marriage symbolizes several things. First, it symbolizes God (rather than the believer) initiating the act of deeply knowing the human spirit of the person to whom he has joined himself. Second, it symbolizes the pleasure both receive in the new relationship. Third, it shows how God is instantly gratified in the love relationship whereas the believer must be brought slowly and carefully to that point of ecstasy.

It also seems obvious that the male "covering" the female with his body, as well as sexual penetration by the male, also establishes a certain appearance of protection as well as pre-eminence of male over the female. This covering and penetration are also symbolic of God as protector and pre-eminent in his relationship to the Church (or to Israel). Yes, even sexual penetration has symbolic meaning to God. This was not an accident of nature. It is how God designed the sexual metaphor. Though penetration does convey a measure of dominance, this is not the kind of domination as defined by some feminists and other non-Christians. Domination in the non-Christian world rarely is mentioned in the same sentence as *love*, since one seems to be the antithesis of the other, and yet love is exactly the kind of domination that God demonstrates to his wife, the Church. We've already seen the words of Paul in Ephesians 5 regarding the husband's love for his wife:

> Husbands love your wives, just as Christ loved the church… In this same way, husbands ought to love their wives as their own bodies. He who loves his wife loves himself.

Paul uses the word *love* five times to describe how the man is to treat his wife. This is how Christian men "dominate" their wives—with love, not with force.

To counter the dominant position of the man in a marriage, God has given the "goddess" of the relationship plenty of power and therefore plenty of control over the male in and out of the bedroom. She has the power to say no, and that's all she should need to keep him in check, if the man respects her refusal. You may think this is pressing symbolism too far, but even the power to say *no* is symbolic. (No, seriously). The woman is symbolic of all mankind, right? So when the Spirit of God approaches a person with whom he would like to have a relationship, what is the one word God hears the most? It's *no*. "No, not now," "No, I'm too busy," "No, I don't feel like it right now," or "No, I have better things to do." When any man or woman says no to God, God cannot and will not violate their decision, and any man who loves his wife as Christ loved the Church would not force himself upon his wife, either. Interpreting this symbolically means God will not "penetrate" their spirit or force himself upon the non-believer (or the believer for that matter); he honors that boundary because he has given mankind the power to make their own decisions. However, most people on Judgment Day may wish they never had that power to resist God, but in fact, they do.

A Feminist's Rejection of God's Sexual Symbolism

Andrea Dworkin fought bitterly against the way God established the sexual relationship between man and woman. She grew up in a Jewish home but obviously didn't believe in the God of the Jewish Bible and clearly didn't like the symbolism behind marriage and the sexual act. She wrote of how the woman was unfairly under the domination of the man, all because of "intercourse." In fact, that was the title of her book on the subject:

> Intercourse…appears to be the key to women's lower human status. By definition, as the God *who does not exist* made her, she is intended to have a lesser privacy, a lesser integrity of the body, a lesser sense of self, since her body can be physically occupied and, in the occupation taken over. By definition, as the God *who does not exist* made her, this lesser privacy, this lesser integrity, this lesser self, establishes her lesser significance: not just in the world of social policy but in the world of bare, true, real existence. She is defined by

how she is made, that hole, which is synonymous
with entry; and intercourse, the act fundamental
to existence, has consequences to her being that
may be intrinsic, not socially imposed.[215]

This is a woman who hated and rejected the way God made her.
She refused to acknowledge God's very existence, but God is the very
reference point by which all her value judgments must be made. If
there were no God, then she would only have the empty universe into
which to scream her complaints. A universe undirected by any purpose
is her only other possible mediator. And it doesn't care that one gender
is dominated by another—that's simply the way a random universe
operates. It's survival of the fittest. But if you want to scream at God,
then you must take into account that he has a *purpose* for placing man
slightly above the woman in some aspects of the human relationship.

God has a stake in this game which is bigger than hurting the
feelings of feminists. God has engineered a mold which, if people
allow themselves to be poured into it, gives them a better chance to
understand God's nature and plan, and a better chance to survive
Judgment Day. The understanding is this: To have a relationship with
God, you must allow God to penetrate your spirit. You must do this
willingly and if you choose not to, that's okay—you just have to live
with the consequences of rejecting your Maker, who wants a love relationship with you. Of course, God runs the great risk of his marriage
metaphor being ruined by divorce, homosexuality, gender confusion,
misguided, abusive husbands, and feminists. Not all young girls are
loved by their fathers, which is where these gender lessons should be
first taught. Fathers are the first ones to see that, compared with their
sons, these beautiful young flowers must travel a gentler path, a path
where they can plant life wherever they go in a world filled with death,
where their beauty and love can shine like a garden in bloom.

In a sinful world, not all women are deeply loved and nurtured
by their husbands, either. God intends that men fully learn the nature
of their wives and how to treat them with love. Here's another clue

---

[215] Dworkin, *Intercourse*, 155, emphasis mine.

for husbands: Never stop *romancing* your wives. This will keep their love for you alive which will bring you many benefits.

Naturally, there are plenty of difficulties that present themselves in a marriage, giving rise to all sorts of conflict, bitterness and division. These things do not come from God but from human failure spurred on by God's enemy, who seeks to destroy all marriage symbolism at every turn and in every marriage, especially those of believers. But these failures do not nullify the basic metaphor that God put in place. A wife submitting to a loving husband is just like what all of us have to do in order to have a loving relationship with God.

If feminists do not like God's symbolism, where a loving husband taking his place as the gentle leader over his wife, willing to give up his life for hers, then they will have to explain why human relationships should be any different from those in the animal kingdom, where domination is the rule of the day. It is only when feminists reject God that they are forced to deal with the alternative, where the strongest survive and seek power and cruel domination over all challengers. Christians do not support this kind of domination, in their sex lives or anywhere else. Jesus clearly taught, "My command is this: Love each other as I have loved you. Greater love has no one than this, that he lay down his life for his friends."[216] The way to "domination" in God's world is by sacrificing and humbling yourself, doing service to those who are in need. Again, Jesus said, "If anyone wants to be first, he must be the very last, and the servant of all."[217]

The kind of "domination" Christian husbands believe in is to treat their wives better than themselves. Feminists should have no argument with a husband who looks to please his wife throughout their relationship. Therefore, just because sexual penetration was created by God to demonstrate God's own pre-eminence and faithful love for his children, the abuse of that purpose on a human level should not be laid at the feet of God, Christians, or anyone else who see sexual roles for what they are—a promise of the husband to over-

---

[216] John 15:12–13.
[217] Mark 9:35.

shadow his wife with love and protection. Abuses will always come, but blaming the Creator when the weak get abused and God's good purposes for a relationship are ignored is *not* his fault.

Seeing Immorality as a Broken Symbol

Sexual symbolism is so important to God that any violation of it (for example, sex outside marriage) draws certain punishment *whether they are Christians or not*. Consider what the apostle Paul wrote to the Thessalonian church:

> It is God's will that you should be sanctified: that you should *avoid sexual immorality*; that each of you should learn to control his own body in a way that is holy and honorable, not in passionate lust like the heathen, who do not *know* God; and that in this matter no one should wrong his brother or take advantage of him. *The Lord will punish men for all such sins, as we have already told you and warned you.* For God did not call us to be impure, but to live a holy life. Therefore, he who rejects this instruction does not reject man but God, who gives you his Holy Spirit.[218]

As if we don't know by now, God punishes people for breaking the symbolism that he has built into his creation. And he has the right to do so. In the NIV translation, the phrase "the Lord will punish" is more accurately translated "the Lord is an avenger," as seen in the English Standard Version:

> Because *the Lord is an avenger* in all these things, as we told you beforehand and solemnly warned you.[219]

---

[218] 1 Thessalonians 4:3–6, New International Version.
[219] 1 Thessalonians 4:6, *The Holy Bible: English Standard Version*.

The Greek word for *avenger* is *ekdikos,* which originally meant "he who by an offense places himself outside the limits of the law."[220] Now what does *that* mean? Leading up to New Testament times, the word took on the meaning of "the avenger who executes a judicial sentence."[221] You could say that God "takes the law into his own hands and punishes the offender." It has to be stressed that when sexual symbolism is broken, God is the *first one offended,* and he will defend his right to avenge himself on the law breaker or, in this case, on the symbol breaker. Paul adds that he has already warned the Thessalonian church of this before. It would be a mistake to interpret Paul's warning as given only to Christians. It most certainly is not. Paul says God is the avenger who will carry out the punishment on anyone ("in *all* these things") for breaking his moral law which, in this case, is the participation in sexual relations outside marriage. Therefore, when a person or society or government breaks a God-given symbol such as one man (normally) marrying one woman, God will punish that person, society, or government. As Paul writes elsewhere,

> Do not be deceived: God cannot be mocked. A man reaps what he sows. The one who sows *to please his sinful nature,* from that nature *will reap destruction*; the one who sows to please the Spirit, from the Spirit will reap eternal life.[222]

And again, the author of the book of Hebrews warns,

> Marriage should be honored by all, and the marriage bed kept pure, for God will judge the adulterer and *all* the sexually immoral.[223]

---

[220] Schrenk, ἐκδικέω, ἔκδικος, ἐκδίκησις, G. Kittel, Bromiley, and Friedrich (eds.), *Theological dictionary of the New Testament,* 442–446.

[221] Ibid.

[222] Galatians 6:7–8

[223] Hebrews 13:4, emphasis mine.

Anyone who seriously believes that America and the West will escape God's judgment for its flagrant sexual immorality is dangerously deceived, and Christians must never give up the fight to maintain holiness both in their own lives and in their interactions with those nonbelievers around them. "For God did not call us to be impure, but to live a holy life."[224] We must also seek to influence the nation's political decisions from the school board to the White House, because if we don't, the immoral will be happy to fill the vacuum.

The short of it is that any sexual inclinations we might have outside marriage must be put down by the power of the Spirit and our affections redirected back to our spouse, or, if we're single, redirected back to God for closer *spiritual* communion with him. Christians, through the power of the Holy Spirit, must maintain sexual purity, especially in this time of gross immorality, approved, proclaimed, and enforced by our own ungodly government even though founded long ago on Christian principles.

Sexuality and Knowing God

When understood in this metaphorical way, the sexual act within marriage is a symbol that God wants to keep pure. Breaking that symbol brings with it the promise of God's retribution. Sexual knowledge has been very specially designed by God as a symbol to draw people closer to each other and to himself. So God seeks out a person with whom to enter into a love relationship. The person receives God's advances through the convicting work of the Holy Spirit. Then they enter into a covenant with God, similar to that of a marriage relationship where they experience God's love now, and ecstasy in the future, every bit as exciting as a love relationship in a new marriage. We will come to know God more and more, until one day we finally see him face to face and there is nothing hidden between us. Then, we literally have all our senses overloaded with pleasure. God himself is rewarded with our undivided worship

---

[224] 1 Thessalonians 4:7.

because we see him for what he truly is: the most loving, forgiving, and *worthy* being ever imagined by the mind of man. He is the greatest husband ever imagined in the dreams of a love-stricken heart of a woman. In this way, marriage is truly mysterious, and if we understand marriage from God's symbolic point of view, it can help us strengthen our own marriages as we model our own relationship after his perfect love toward us.

Standing against Hedonism

Sexual pleasure is completely pure and holy in God's eyes for those bound by marriage. Sex should never be thought of as dirty or sinful inside that context. Outside marriage, sexual pleasures are always sinful and unholy, but in the present age, that notion is complete nonsense. The reason for the hedonistic position that sex is okay at any time, any place lies in the complete misunderstanding of God's reasons for restricting this pleasure. It is up to Bible-believing Christians first to maintain their own self-control and second to be a moral light in an ever-darkening world, upholding the vital symbolism God has placed in the sexual union. As Paul said, "Have nothing to do with the fruitless deeds of darkness, but rather expose them. For it is shameful even to mention what the disobedient do in secret."[225]

If everyone listening to Jesus left the area when he told them they had to drink his blood and eat his flesh, they would surely flee to the mountains after hearing God's ideas behind sexual symbolism. Still, we must be firm in our commitment to uphold all of God's truths. Knowing how God thinks is the first step. Passing it on to our children is the next. There is a great risk that casting these pearls to the swine of this generation will unleash great hatred toward Christianity and the Bible. We should expect it. But we must do what we can to take back that lost ground and never flinch at upholding the sexual symbolism that God has established.

---

[225] Ephesians 5:11–12.

14

Marital Confusion

For this reason a man will leave his father and
mother and be united to his wife, and the two
will become one flesh.' So they are no longer
two, but one. Therefore, what God has joined
together, let man not separate.

—the Lord Jesus Christ, Matthew 19:4–6

B iblical symbolism, especially the male-female distinction, has
played such a vast role in shaping Western society that Christians
believed those foundations would be in place forever. Now that those
norms have been nearly destroyed by the enemies of God, both human
and demonic, believers are left looking for a way forward. That way is
to relearn what the Bible does and does not say about sex, gender, and
marriage, which has been the bedrock of western civilization and the
reason for our prosperity under God's hand. A fresh understanding of
marriage symbolism provides the biblical absolutes necessary to judge
between truth and error in our morally corrupt culture.

Attacks on Biblical Marriage

Marriage has been under attack for a long time. A few years
back, three scholars put forth a novel attack on the traditional definition of marriage in an op-ed column in an Iowa newspaper, the
Des Moines Register. That definition *should* have been one man and

one woman in a covenant before God. The column was picked up by another progressive news source, the *Huffington Post* website. One of its associates, Meredith Bennett-Smith, was working at the time for *HuffPost*. Bennett-Smith, a left-wing, pro-homosexual activist, interviewed one of the authors of the opinion piece, Iowa University's Robert R. Cargill, and published parts of that interview online under the title "Biblical Marriage Not Defined Simply As One Man, One Woman: Iowa Religious Scholars' Op-Ed."[226] She commented on Cargill's argument thus:

> The Bible's definition of marriage can be confusing and contradictory, noted the scholars. <u>They stated in their column</u>[227] that a primary example of this is <u>the religious book's stance on polygamy</u>,[228] a practice that was embraced by prominent biblical figures Abraham and David.[229]

As is frequently done, even by some scholars, Cargill committed a logical fallacy. He argued from an almost-valid *particular* observation and used it to support an *invalid, universal* conclusion. More on that in a minute.

Now, Christians do need to be exact when arguing about the definition of marriage from Scripture. So what exactly is the correct definition of marriage and why did Cargill seem to have a valid point regarding polygamy, perhaps requiring an expansion of the definition of marriage? From Genesis 2:24, we know that God's perfect idea of marriage was, in fact, between one man and one woman. The act of man leaving father and mother, cleaving to his wife and becoming one flesh is the very definition of marriage. So why did some prom-

---

[226] Bennett-Smith, retrieved July 16, 2016.
[227] http://friendlyatheist.patheos.com/2013/06/05/biblical-scholars-actually-traditional-marriage-isnt-just-one-man-and-one-woman/
[228] http://usatoday30.usatoday.com/news/opinion/columnist/2004-10-03-turley_x.htm
[229] Bennett-Smith.

inent Bible figures get away with having multiple wives and concubines? In a word, the reason is *sin*—well, sin and economics.

Polygamy and Divorce

Men in Biblical times loved the pleasures of a woman every bit as much as they do today. And if a man had the means to support other wives and cultural laws permitted it, the man could take multiple wives. Having additional wives and therefore more children (read: *workers*) in a hardscrabble, primitive existence in ancient times, a man could increase his wealth and live more comfortably (albeit amid the squabbling and petty jealousies among the wives). But this doesn't fully answer the question of why God *permitted* this arrangement. Make no mistake—while God didn't design it, God did *permit* it. In fact, he put laws in place through Moses (living well after the time of Abraham) which made sure that an unloved wife or concubine in a polygamous relationship was not treated unfairly.[230] God did this because he is a God of love and fairness and he looked with compassion on a wife or concubine who was ignored or mistreated. God actually gave them written rights in a world where, in many other cultures, there were no such rights to be had. Polygamy may not have originated with God, but in Mosaic law, he made sure it wouldn't be abused, at least, not in Israel.

In the same way, God directed Moses to *permit* (by law) the man to divorce his wife.[231] In fact, even *that* is overstating God's involvement with divorce. God actually never gave a law *directing* anyone to divorce. Divorce was already in place among the people when God first made any mention of it in Leviticus 21:7, where he directed those in the priestly class, "They must not marry women defiled by prostitution or *divorced* from their husbands, because priests are holy to their God." Divorce is broken symbolism and was invented by the will of man, not the will of God. Jesus truly said, "Moses *permitted* you to divorce your wives because your hearts were hard. But it was

---

[230] Deuteronomy 21:15–17.
[231] Deuteronomy 24:1

not this way from the beginning."[232] So even there, the Lord Jesus said divorce was in the law by *permission*, not by a direct commandment from God. Jesus hearkened back to Genesis and confirmed that God's will was for one man to marry one woman and that God himself is the one who joined the two together. Once again, because of man's sinful condition, even Jesus, speaking from the Father, realized that not everyone would be able to accept that teaching. That said, Jesus did exempt the case of marital unfaithfulness[233] in his teaching against divorce, perhaps allowing that it was the sexual sin which broke the symbolism of marriage, not the divorce afterward. Regardless, God still makes his heart known to us in Malachi 2:16, where he said without qualification, "I *hate* divorce." Because of the hardness of our hearts (which, at its root, is unforgiveness), Jesus allowed that this was a hard teaching, that whoever *could* accept this difficult law *should* accept it, realizing that not all had the same commitment to their spouse that God has toward his covenant people. Even so, there were complaints about this new understanding of marriage from his closest disciples.

Marital unfaithfulness is the only legitimate reason permitted by God to pursue a divorce. God himself actually did send Israel, his own wife, away to Assyria because she "cheated" on him by worshiping all the gods of the surrounding nations. Jeremiah records, "I gave faithless Israel her certificate of divorce and sent her away because of all her adulteries."[234] God, in effect, divorced Israel because she broke symbolism by acting as though there was some problem with God when really the problem was her own unfaithfulness. God also sent the southern kingdom of Judah away to Babylon for seventy years because of their unfaithfulness. During that time most of the offenders had died in Babylon and the Land had its rest from the constant lawbreaking of its people. After that, God drew many people back to the land of Judah where the nation and its relationship to God began to be rebuilt. God can and does forgive those who commit

---

[232] Matthew 19:8.

[233] Greek *porneia*, or sexual immorality, not Greek *moichao* which is the word used for adultery specifically involving a *married* woman.

[234] Jeremiah 3:8.

adultery against him but there must be punishment for breaking the symbolism of God as the faithful husband to unfaithful Israel. Even now, Israel is in the early stages of restoration after a long period of separation—one could call it divorce—from God for rejecting Jesus as their promised Messiah.

Taken together, laws regulating polygamy and divorce did not change the one-man-one-woman definition of marriage and did not harm the symbolism God intended to portray by the institution. Rather, God took man's sinful nature into account when he gave the laws to Moses regulating marriage, polygamy, and divorce.

Polyandry

A more interesting question is, Why didn't God permit *polyandry* in the Law of Moses? Polyandry is the practice of a wife having two or more husbands at the same time. The reason polyandry wasn't permitted but polygamy was is this: symbolism. God is the husband to both Israel and the Church—and in a more granular way, the husband to each individual believer. God is the model for marriage. Marriage is symbolic of God's relationship to us. Since he himself is the husband to many "wives" or many believers, it therefore does not violate *symbolism* for a human male to have multiple wives. It may violate other standards, such as fairness between the wives, equal treatment between the children, and a man's basic sanity, but it doesn't specifically violate the symbolism between God and the plural nature of his wife (that is, those believers who are committed to him). However, just because it doesn't violate symbolism does not mean that God intended polygamy as a norm for human marriage. It simply means that God is not offended at the *idea* of polygamy. It is not twisted, detestable or an abomination to his character, and it does not break the symbol of human marriage as he designed it. Again, polygamy was not God's idea; it was already in place at the time God gave Moses the commandments, and so God regulated against its abuse. Polygamy, in and of itself, does not violate the symbolism behind God's character. Polyandry does.

God is a realist when it comes to sinful human nature. In the Old Testament, God permitted the practice of polygamy since it didn't violate the symbolism of his character. In the New Testament, and in the Western world where Christianity has flourished, monogamy has also flourished. When Jesus spoke against divorce, he also seemed to reiterate the practice of monogamy when he said, "at the beginning the Creator 'made them male and female.'" [235] In God's eyes, this raised the value of women to that of equality with men. At the same time, the symbolism behind monogamy emphasized the believer's individual importance to God since it demonstrated the husband's singular focus on one woman. Polyandry, in symbolic terms, would be the same as saying that a human being (though he or she is a "wife" of God and betrothed to him) can still worship and be committed to *other* gods as well, alongside their true husband (i.e., Jehovah). Worshiping Jehovah equally alongside other gods (i.e., other "husbands") is idolatry and is roundly condemned by the first commandment: *You shall have no other gods before me.*[236] Polyandry is an abomination to God's symbolic way of thinking.

Friends with Benefits: Polyamory

In today's world where marriage has become optional, another form of replacement partnership has emerged: multiple friends with benefits. There is, of course, great benefit in having strong, close friendships. But when those friendships turn romantic and then sexual, you have aroused God's role as avenger. Sexual pleasure was only meant to be a fulfillment, a reward, a gift to those in a committed relation of one man, one woman. Remember the marriage formula: leave home, be committed to your spouse, and become one flesh. Governments have added other requirements to simplify their efforts of governing, but those do not alter God's mandate. If a married couple allows a female friend to live with them, you do not *automatically* have a polyamorous relationship. You simply have an unwise

---

[235] Matthew 19:4–6.
[236] Exodus 20:3.

arrangement, tailor-made for Satan's handiwork. Satan will do his best to push the menagerie forward until the marriage covenant and its symbolism is broken.

How about a married couple bringing in a male friend? What could possibly go wrong there? If the husband has already signaled his willingness to give up the couple's privacy, it's only a few short steps away from complete disaster. The mandate to believers is to avoid all appearance of evil. This is to avoid Satan's temptations, followed by falling headlong into sin, followed by God's judgment.

The symbolism is simple. God makes a covenant with anyone who is willing to receive Jesus as Lord and Savior. The new believer may not even know what it *means* to receive Jesus as Lord. Just having him as Savior is enough for the moment. But it's a package deal. Jesus not only saves us from eternal punishment for sin, he also leads us in a lifelong exercise to overcome all sin in this life. That requires him to be Lord over us as well. Someone who receives Jesus as Savior but steadfastly refuses him as Lord likely never had him as Savior. Having Jesus as Lord is the best thing that could ever have happened to us. He knows what's best. Now, back to the broken symbolism of polyamory. God has the capacity to have infinite believers in a covenant relationship with him, and he is able to satisfy the needs of every one as though they were the *only* one. Human husbands (and wives) do not have that capability. In his wisdom, God designed a one-woman, one-man relationship. No doubt there are special circumstances where godly people have the need to shelter one or more friends temporarily, but this should not be for the purpose of having an ongoing romantic relationship with the guest. We are not to give ground to the Enemy. Nonbelievers who insist on polyamorous relationships will pay the penalty. God is the avenger of broken symbolism.

You Weren't So Bad After All

God never permitted polyandry in Israel and never gave Moses any commands regarding that relationship. The closest thing to it is where God gave Moses a law that prevented a woman from later returning to the husband who divorced her, if in the interim, she had taken another husband (and then was rejected by him as well).[237] So even having one husband at a time and returning to her original husband is still detestable to God because this translates symbolically into something like this: A human male or female enters a marriage covenant with God but then rejects him and chases after another religion or idol and defiles themselves with the god of *that* religion. Then the person has a change of heart again and says, "All things considered, after I've shopped around, I think I like Jehovah better than Baal or Ashtoreth or Chemosh (all of whom are servants of Satan), so I'll go back to the *true* God and serve him again. God calls that *detestable* in Deuteronomy 24:4. Why is it detestable? Because it's *insulting* to God to leave him in the first place, thinking some better god can be found and then returning to the true God after spiritually defiling themselves with the practices of the lesser god. Do you remember when Jesus asked the disciples, "Will you leave too?" when many others left after a particularly difficult teaching? Peter answered, "Lord, to whom shall we go? You have the words of eternal life."[238] It breaks symbolism and is offensive to God for anyone to hold the true God as equal to other demonic beings or gods.

Life for us isn't a big beauty contest where we get to choose among God and all the other idols and demons available to us from other religions, then hold up a scorecard with a number from 1 through 10 on it, telling God where we think he fits on our scale of approval. The one true God is the most amazing, most loving, most powerful, most faithful, most protective God around. There is no other power in this universe or any other being who compares with our God and his Son, Jesus Christ. If any believer leaves God for some other god, idol, pet, hobby, or anything else, he or she has some serious explaining to do on Judgment Day. As if that isn't amazing enough, a human being actually can leave God in this age, perform the detestable act of dedicating him or herself to some other god, person, or activity, and then later return in dedication to the true God, and God will forgive and accept that person back again. He will overlook the insult and wel-

---

[237] Deuteronomy 24:1–4; Jeremiah 3:1.
[238] John 6:68.

come them back with open arms, just like the father of the prodigal son.[239] But God doesn't want to elevate or establish this behavior in the human realm or pretend this to be normal human behavior even though it does happen in real life. It's just another example of detestable human behavior with a little less penalty attached to it.

Is That a Guy or a Girl?

Another example of detestable gender symbolism occurs in Deuteronomy 22:5, where God forbids cross-dressing. He forbids it because he doesn't want the lines crossed between the male who represents God and the female who represents the believer in God. The roles were never meant to be crossed when God created male and female and to do so by crossdressing shows a misunderstanding of the symbolism that God designed for each. Blurring those lines is the first step toward crossing the line. Pity the children whose parents neglect to teach little boys how to be young men and little girls how to grow up as young women. Dressing boys and girls differently is the first step in this instruction. There are, naturally, societal differences in the way people dress, but most, if not all, cultures make *some* differentiation between male and female clothing. Parents need to make the distinctions clear so there is no confusion for the children later in life. In the unfortunate case where a baby is born with deformed genitals or even both sets of genitals, the parents should raise their child according to the gender determined at birth by the chromosomes in their DNA. A male child has an XY chromosome pair while a female child has an XX chromosome pair. It's so simple there should be no confusion. But Satan is alive and well.

Breaking Symbolism: The Cause of Confusion

Now back to Cargill. He said that the biblical rules surrounding marriage are confused and contradictory. The real source of confusion, however, comes from his inability to recognize the symbolism

---

[239] Luke 15:11–32.

behind God's regulations on marriage. He doesn't understand why God says it's okay to permit *some* contrary behaviors but not others. Polygamy does add a certain amount of confusion if you leave symbolism out of the equation. But that still doesn't condone Cargill's move when he starts with a particular thesis—that polygamy confuses the marriage definition—and then jumps to an illogical, universal conclusion—therefore many relationships, including same-sex marriage, are permissible. Consider this next statement from Cargill, how God's acceptance of polygamy allows the possibility of alternatives to the "one man, one woman" definition of marriage:

> He [Cargill] explained that it is obvious to scholars (and some religious leaders) that the Bible *endorses* a wide range of relationships.[240]

The Bible *does not endorse a wide range of relationships,* if by "wide," you mean to include same-sex marriage, which is what Cargill and some other scholars are really arguing for. God allowed some imperfect interactions such as polygamy and divorce to be legislated, but only those relationships that do not violate his holy character that he designed symbolically into Adam and Eve at the time of creation.

You can see where Cargill is headed. If the definition of marriage is not between one man and one woman *in all cases,* that leaves the door open, not only for polygamy (which does not do violence to his character) but also for all kinds of perverted relationships that *do* violate his character, such as homosexuality, lesbianism, gender modification, and all the other letters of the gender alphabet as well, all fully endorsed by moral authorities such as Cargill, some scholars, Bennett-Smith, and the *Huffington Post.* In fact, the next quote from Cargill takes the final step toward his objective:

> Ultimately, said Cargill, a Biblical "argument against same-sex marriage is wholly unsustainable. We all know this, but very few scholars are

---

[240] Bennett-Smith. op cit., emphasis mine.

talking about it, because they don't want to take the heat."[241]

First, an argument against same-sex marriage is not *wholly unsustainable*. This is a complete logical fallacy. You can't reason directly from the premise that "one man-one woman is too narrow" all the way to "therefore lots of other marriage combinations are valid as well, including same-sex marriage." That would be like saying the following:

1. God said "You shall not murder."
2. That law is too restrictive since God commanded Noah to put all murderers to death.
3. Therefore, God should allow a wide variety of killing.

That is weak reasoning. The only thing evident from the reasoning of Cargill is that he, and scholars who side with him, have no idea under the sun how God thinks. By now, all the readers of this book know that God thinks *in symbols*. What *is* wholly unsustainable is imagining that God left some kind of ambiguity in his definition of marriage that could only be untangled by scholars who can now tell us what God *really* meant about marriage. That's what is wholly unsustainable. And to say that "all scholars know this"—meaning there is no sustainable, biblical argument against same-sex marriage—this means only one thing: these so-called scholars don't *know* anything.

Christians must realize that God has a fixed nature which doesn't change directions with the wind like liberal theology. He has reasons for everything he says. It is better to stand in solidarity with Scriptural values, even when we might not fully understand them, rather than abandon God's principles in favor of the godless reasoning from the scholars of the day who will answer for their twisted logic on Judgment Day. It's also better to understand how God thinks so that, when error comes around, the believer can spot

---

[241] Bennett-Smith.

it a mile away. And, in the case of same-sex marriage, we *do* know why God is against it—*symbolism*. But he is also loving, faithful, and forgiving. He is always welcoming of anyone previously caught up in any sexual sin who sincerely desires to leave the demonic confusion of his or her past life. They can then begin to follow God through the power of the Holy Spirit, who is our only hope for overcoming these very real and potentially addicting sexual perversions. His forgiveness comes without measure to those who believe in Jesus. This is the basis for a new hope which is a life lived for Jesus Christ and in his great power. Cargill and his fellow scholars need to repent and re-read the Bible, allowing God to be the judge of what does or does not violate his own character.

15

Detestable Symbolism

Everyone who does any of these detestable things—such persons must be cut off from their people.

—Leviticus 18:29

The Israelites, led by Moses in the wilderness, were being prepared by God to take over the land of Canaan. This occurred from about 1450 through 1410 BC.[242] They were to drive out the wicked inhabitants of that land who were doing detestable things in God's sight, breaking very important symbols that God intended for Israel and the world to understand and respect. They were also warned not to repeat the sins of the Canaanites, else they would suffer the same fate. What were these detestable acts? What offended God so much that many thousands of human beings were literally to be destroyed, including men, women, children, and sometimes even animals? God listed for the Israelites many of those detestable acts in several sections of the book of Leviticus known as the "Holiness Code," comprising chapters 17–26, but especially in chapter 18.

Leviticus is a book about spiritual holiness and its earthly counterpart, proper human behavior such as family relations, diet, and cleanliness. The practices of the Canaanites dishonored God's rela-

---

[242] Elwell and Comfort, *Timeline of Biblical Events,* in *Tyndale Bible Dictionary,* 1337.

tionship to man by destroying the intended symbolism behind matters like worship, marriage, and the dignity of human sexuality. If the magnitude of heaven and earth showed anything at all, it showed that God is great, that there is none greater, and that he is due the respect and worship of all his created beings. The abuse of God's design for creation, such as the unholy practices of the Canaanites, will always draw punishment and often, quite severe punishment. Understanding the symbolism behind these detestable acts will go a long way toward understanding how God thinks, hopefully with the result of gaining a better relationship with the God who made us.

How the Canaanites Dishonored God

The offenses outlined in the Holiness Code cover a wide-ranging collection of issues such as the meaning and improper use of blood, including pagan sacrifices, a woman's purification, and the prohibition on eating blood. Also included: immoral sexual relations, various forms of witchcraft and incestuous marriages. All these things (and more) had three things in common. First, they all violated God's holiness and the laws that symbolized that holiness. Those symbols had a meaning so deeply held by God that he could not allow such a violator of those laws in Israel to live. Second, very few of these practices would offend any modern-day person. In fact, most people today would be horrified that God himself would level such harsh punishment against any human being. The last thing these offenses had in common is that God is still offended by them today, nearly 3,500 years later.

Incestuous Marriages

God is dishonored when close family members are joined in marriage. Consider the verse "No one is to approach any close relative to have sexual relations. I am the Lord."[243] This is an introduction to several verses in Leviticus 18 about having sexual relations within

---

[243] Leviticus 18:6.

the extended family, which God saw as detestable behavior. These laws of consanguinity are still nearly universal to this day and were put in place to prevent this important symbolism of marriage from being minimized by marrying one's parents, children, aunts, uncles, and other close relations. The metaphorical implication seems to be that God, as husband, would not seek an intimate relationship with someone just because they are related to a worshiper of God. Every worshiper becomes a member of God's "wife" or "bride" as an individual worshiper, not as part of a family or based on someone else's relationship to God.

In addition to breaking marriage symbolism, we now know that human marriage with close relatives can cause certain genetic diseases to develop in the children of these relationships. In Leviticus 18, the following family members are forbidden to marry:

- daughter
- stepchildren
- aunt
- sister or half sister
- stepsisters
- daughter-in-law
- granddaughter
- step-granddaughter

Cousins and second cousins are permitted to marry, as far as the Law of Moses is concerned. Today, about half of the states in the US prohibit cousin marriage. Marrying a first cousin is also permitted in the UK.[244]

Detestable Idol Worship

Other broken symbols, such as the worship of other gods, were so detestable to God that even the gold and silver used to fashion these

---

[244] "Focus on the Family," *Cousin Marriage*, retrieved March 1, 2019.

"graven images" were to be utterly destroyed by fire.[245] Sometimes, these religions even required offering one's children as burnt offerings to some demonic god,[246] rather than a sheep or other animal, as the Lord commanded.

Blood Symbolism

God created all life. He designed the blood molecule to deliver oxygen and other nutrients to every cell of a living body as well as to carry away carbon dioxide and other waste materials for disposal by other bodily organs designed for that purpose. Deep in God's mind, it pleased him that the blood sacrifice of an animal (which to him represented life) satisfied his desire for honor in the face of human sin. Obeying that command and offering that sacrifice was an act of honoring God. The symbolic message behind that command was fulfilled. That message was that God was willing to trade innocent blood for the forgiveness of the guilty. Likewise, it was an act of dishonor to disobey any of the other Levitical sacrificial laws.[247] The penalty for such dishonor to God was the death of the sinner, since that person rejected the only prescribed method of forgiveness. As described before, God told Moses, "The life of the flesh is in the blood...for it is the blood by reason of the life that makes atonement."[248]

The symbolism behind blood, however, goes even deeper. Since blood represents life, in God's mind, there is also deep symbolism regarding the blood of a woman's womb. According to Genesis 3:20, Eve was "the mother of all the living." Her monthly flow of blood represented, in part, the life force that God gave women when he created Eve. When a woman ovulates but does not become pregnant, blood and tissue are discharged from the womb and she became ceremonially unclean for seven days[249] while her body cleansed itself. God intended to keep this uncleanness a private matter between her

---

[245] Deuteronomy 7:25–26.

[246] Leviticus 18:21.

[247] Leviticus 7:27; 17:7, 8.

[248] Leviticus 17:11

[249] Leviticus 15:19.

and God. As it is written, "If a man lies with a woman during her monthly period and has sexual relations with her, he has exposed the source of her flow, and she has also uncovered it. Both of them must be cut off from their people."[250] God therefore sees this act as a violation or corruption of the woman's source of life. He again felt strongly enough about it to assign the death penalty to the man and the woman for breaking his command.

Again, this has deep symbolic meaning to the God who designed all human life. This symbolism was meant never to be broken, not even in modern times. Although no longer considered a death-penalty offense by any modern culture, the principle behind the command still reveals how God feels about this violation. It also affords the woman a time, protected from the desires of her husband, where she can reflect with God on her amazing ability to bring life into the world, painful as that might sometimes be.

Other Detestable Actions

There were many other things done by the Canaanites that were detestable to God, each demanding the death penalty if committed by any Israelite. This applied to adultery,[251] witchcraft,[252] cursing one's father or mother,[253] "lying with a man as one lies with a woman,"[254] and having sexual relations with animals.[255] All those things (among others) were death-penalty offenses in Mosaic law. They all broke either the symbolism behind true worship of a holy God, or respect for human dignity or other parts of God's creation. God made it crystal clear that for his people to be holy, they had to be set apart from the surrounding nations. They were not to act like

---

[250] Leviticus 20:18.
[251] Leviticus 18:20.
[252] Deuteronomy 18:10.
[253] Leviticus 20:9.
[254] Leviticus 18:22.
[255] Leviticus 18:23.

the Canaanites, whom God was driving out of their land, or like any other heathen people. God said to them,

> [Y]ou must not do any of these detestable things, for all these things were done by the people who lived in the land before you, and the land became defiled. And if you defile the land, it will vomit you out as it vomited out the nations that were before you. Everyone who does any of these detestable things—such persons must be cut off from their people.[256]

We can understand the reasoning behind punishing some of these practices, such as child sacrifice (although modern-day abortion serves the same purpose of disposing of unwanted infants). But other commands require a little more investigation to fully understand why God was angered when they were broken, especially at a time when Western nations that formerly stood firmly on the principles of God's Word now fully support some of the most detestable practices.

Lying with a Man as with a Woman

Today, homosexuality seems to have been accepted as an alternative lifestyle by much of the modern world. Yet the reason God finds this behavior detestable has not changed. The reason male homosexuality is detestable to God is that critical symbolism designed into human marriage is violated. Worse, the insult falls back upon God himself. Two distortions about marriage are made clear when considering the Greek words for male homosexuality listed in a group of condemned activities in 1 Corinthians 6:9–11. Since homosexuality has been around since ancient times, more than one language, including New Testament Greek, had words to describe each side of the homosexual relationship. When two men join themselves sexu-

---

[256] Leviticus 18:26–29

ally, invariably one man by default plays the role of "passive partner," a role that God never intended for the man to play. The other participant plays the role of the "active partner," the usual role for the male. *Malakos* is the Greek word that represents the passive partner. The Greek-English Lexicon of the New Testament states that *malakos* is

> the passive male partner in homosexual intercourse—"homosexual…" As in Greek, a number of other languages also have entirely distinct terms for the active and passive roles in homosexual intercourse.[257]

God designed the male (in a perfect world) to be the "stronger" partner in a marriage. Many people, even Christians, don't believe or understand *why* homosexual behavior is detestable to God. Having a man pose as the weaker partner in a sexual union is a corruption of the symbolism God intended for marriage. Therefore, the proper picture of God as a strong but considerate husband lovingly taking a weaker human as his "wife" is completely distorted. Even though one man in a same-sex relationship is *playing* the role of the weaker partner, in God's eyes, these are two equals in a perverted relationship. There is no covenant relationship, there is no "God figure" taking to himself a weaker partner so she can be blessed by God and deeply loved by him. The symbolism of man as representative of God to a weaker and beloved wife is the only valid way to interpret the sexual relationship in human marriage. It supersedes the perversion of two males in a sexual relationship, whether one male is active, passive or equal to any other male.

Remember the symbolism: God is the stronger partner in the covenant relationship to a human being. He penetrates the heart of the human—the weaker partner. Likewise, the man was designed to be the stronger partner in human marriage. That's not to say that there can't be playful interaction between man and woman where either one plays the stronger partner. But ultimately, during inter-

---

[257] Louw and Nida, *Greek-English Lexicon of the New Testament*, ref. 88–281.

course, the male was designed by God to be stronger. A man was never intended to play the role of the passive sexual partner in a marriage. This also is the reason for God's prohibition on men cross-dressing in the Old Testament. God said, "A woman must not wear men's clothing, nor a man wear women's clothing, for the Lord your God detests anyone who does this."[258] This principle may also be applied to another current day perversion: a woman playing the role of a dominatrix in a sexual relationship. It doesn't take much imagination to understand why God might be dishonored by that behavior. A man playing the submissive role in a marital or sexual relationship when he should be exhibiting qualities more becoming to a stronger, more godlike role model is exactly the reason *why* homosexuality is an abomination in God's mind when considering the role of the passive homosexual male.

Active Male Homosexuality

The second great error in homosexuality is seen in the second Greek word used by Paul in the 1st Corinthians 6 passage. This word is "*arsenokoitai*," defined as

> a male partner in homosexual intercourse—"homosexual..." It is possible that [*arsenokoites*] in certain contexts refers to the *active male partner* in homosexual intercourse in contrast with [*malakos*], the passive male partner.[259]

So this is the more aggressive partner in the male-on-male relationship. As we have seen, God is the stronger, more active male figure in *celestial* marriage with all mankind as the weaker partner. He expects the male in a human marriage to be the stronger one as well, when compared with the woman. A male was designed to seek out a

---

[258] Deuteronomy 22:5
[259] Louw and Nida, *Greek-English Lexicon of the New Testament*, ref. 88.280, emphasis mine.

covenant relationship with a weaker being, the female. Male seeking female is a microcosm of God's pursuit of all weaker human beings, male *and* female. On the human level, that symbolism is destroyed by homosexuality. But on a cosmic level, God is profaned in an even deeper way.

To try to make sense out of the broken symbolism of the active male homosexual on a celestial level, the reasoning would go something like this: having two males in a sexual bond would be like God *intimately* joining himself in a covenant to an equal where no such equal exists. Since the only being even remotely equal to God in strength was Lucifer (now Satan), one can understand why any suggestion of an intimate, covenant relationship with Satan is an abomination to God. In Satan's twisted, perverted mind, homosexuality represents Satan's equality to God. Again, Lucifer was God's creation, not his equal. There are other deities who have sought to be equal to God in the past, such as the god at the top of the Greek pantheon, Zeus, all of whom, according to the Apostle Paul, are mythical representations of demons.[260] All those who seek to make themselves equal to God are fit only for destruction, not for a covenant of love with the only true God, they are competitors for the love and affection God desires to give to his spiritual wife. As seen before in the book of Ezekiel, God spoke words of judgment against the Prince of Tyre (most likely possessed by Satan) because that king thought he was a "god:"

> Because you think you are wise,
> as wise as a god,
> I am going to bring foreigners against you,
> the most ruthless of nations;
> they will draw their swords against your beauty
> and wisdom
> and pierce your shining splendor.
> They will bring you down to the pit,
> and you will die a violent death
> in the heart of the seas.

---

[260] 1 Corinthians 10:20.

Will you then say, "I am a god,"
in the presence of those who kill you?
You will be but a man, not a god,
in the hands of those who slay you.
You will die the death of the uncircumcised
at the hands of foreigners.[261]

To imagine God embracing an enemy who claims to be an equal is the very pinnacle of abomination and stands at the heart of God's disgust with active-partner homosexuality. God hates broken symbols, and I think he has a deep emotional hatred for this one, especially since it involves his personal, holy character. Through the symbolism of homosexuality, Satan has accomplished what he set out to do: he made himself equal to God.

Human marriage clues us in on how God has chosen to relate to mankind. It is not inherently unreasonable for God to create one gender as stronger than another (as long as love and mutual consideration are operating in the marriage). The only human sexual relationship endorsed by God is between a married man and his wife. The pleasure received by the female from the physical relationship is symbolic of the spiritual pleasure humans receive from an intimate relationship with God. It also shows that God himself as husband receives some amount of pleasure in return from his spiritual bride—that is, from those worshipers devoted to him. Active male homosexuality, when looked at symbolically, means that God is unwilling to seek out a weaker partner and relate to her on that basis. Instead, he only seeks the strongest of the strong, those who labor to be equal to him. This is the *opposite* of God's idea of marriage, either celestial or earthly. Repentance from this sin is the only way back to a proper relationship with God.

Finally, a word about the three Persons of the Trinity. The Father, Son, and Holy Spirit are one God. In Deuteronomy 6:4 this is made clear: "Hear, O Israel: The Lord our God, the Lord is one." The perfect love that exists between the members of the Trinity is pure, holy

---

[261] Ezekiel 28:6-10.

and perfect. There is no need for a covenant between them because they are already one. So it would be invalid to express their relationship in terms of human marriage. Homosexuality is a corruption of human marriage and God's relationship to human beings. It is not a corruption of the relationship between the members of the Trinity.

Further, the idea that Jesus was a homosexual—a report started as early as the 1500s,[262] is impossible since Jesus lived a completely holy life as a member of the Trinity, saying and doing only the things the Father told him to say and do.[263] It is not possible for God to break his own symbolism, except maybe in one case (which is discussed later). Even then, God himself is willing to accept the insult and dishonor of his own symbolism being broken.

Lesbianism

Male homosexuality gets gender symbolism all wrong. So does lesbianism. In God's mind, the female symbolically represents all believers in their relationship to God (who is their husband). Therefore, two women bound together in a sexual relationship—one could call it a covenant relationship—rejecting a male as their husband, represents *pure humanism* to God. By *humanism* we mean mankind in all their strength, defining their existence totally apart from any consideration of God. Humanism has at its core the belief in their own ability to live independently from God. Lesbianism is a sinful perversion based in idolatry, lust and self-worship like its male counterpart. However, lesbianism doesn't threaten or insult the symbolism of God's character in the same way that male homosexuality does because the female in the relationship doesn't *represent* God, she represents mankind. Or, you could say lesbianism represents mankind in love with itself (hence, humanism). It still represents a rejection of God, but that's just what humanism is at its core—a rejection of one's need for God.

---

[262] Dickson, "Spy Report That Criticised Marlowe for 'Gay Christ' Claim Is Revealed Online," *Guardian*, accessed March 4, 2019.
[263] John 14:24, 31.

God does, however, express revulsion toward male homosexuality and assigns it the death penalty under Mosaic law. While also having disgust for lesbianism, he does not legislate against it. If every act of rejecting God were immediately met with the death penalty, there would be no one left alive upon the earth. This does not mean that God permits female sexual unions in Mosaic law or approves of them in any way. But it does mean that since the death penalty is not prescribed for female homosexuality, God must look at the symbolism behind such activity somewhat differently. The women engaging in this behavior do more to dishonor themselves than they do God. In any case, homosexuality, whether male or female, is a violation of God's holy character.

Relations against Natural Law

The Apostle Paul does speak of all homosexuality (both male and female) as being "against nature." But while lesbianism dishonors mankind because of its humanistic perversion, male homosexuality dishonors God because it shows him to be desirous only of relationships with those claiming equality with him rather than with the needy and weak whom he created and who, in their weakness, need him most.

The human sexual nature, along with its natural opposite-gender attraction, was engineered by God in order to provide a form of moral guardrails in order to keep humanity and the whole plant and animal kingdom moving along in a manageable uniformity throughout all the generations of history. It's the reason why men are sexually attracted to *human* females rather than females of some other species. In the past, God jumped into action when this design faced destruction from his enemy who is also at work *against* the general uniformity God placed within all nature. God showed this decisive action after man's sin in the Garden, and again just before the Flood of Noah, where God hit the reset button, putting an end to all humanity except for the eight members of Noah's family. God also took decisive action against the sexual perversion of Sodom and Gomorrah in about 2067 BC, some 650 years before God led Israel into battle under Joshua against the nearby Canaanites. The Bible confirms this action in Jude 7:

> In a similar way, Sodom and Gomorrah and the surrounding towns gave themselves up to sexual immorality and perversion. They serve as an example of those who suffer the punishment of eternal fire.

Under the ancient law of xenia (pronounced zenEEya) where travellers were guaranteed safe passage when taken in by a local resident, the men of Sodom broke every rule of hospitality in the book when they sought to forcibly rape the visiting angels taken in by Abraham's nephew, Lot. Again, these sins are not just against God's character, but also against nature itself as God created it.

Paul spoke generally about this natural law in mankind in Romans 2:14–15:

> Indeed, when Gentiles, who do not have the law, do *by nature* things required by the law, they are a law for themselves, even though they do not have the law, since they show that the requirements of the law are *written on their hearts*, their consciences also bearing witness, and their thoughts now accusing, now even defending them.

This reference to law being "written on their hearts" is how Paul could earlier speak of men and women abandoning "natural relations" and men committing indecent acts with one another and women doing the same thing with other women in Romans 1.[264]

When human government ceases to uphold natural law marriage, which God defines as one man (Adam) and one woman (Eve), society will eventually break down and cease to operate the way God designed it. Since the godly symbolism behind marriage no longer has

---

[264] Romans 1:24–27.

a hold on the human conscience in our day, many men and women do not receive the same grace from God that leads each of them to a deeper understanding of who God is, hopefully followed by salvation and a renewed relationship with the Creator. It's because of sin that our consciences can be corrupted by the Enemy and dragged off into various perversions. Satan does not want anything to go "according to plan," especially when it's God's plan. The result of such perversion is punishment, preferably by human government upholding God's laws, but when human government refuses to guard God's character, God has other methods of punishment at his disposal such as the breakdown of societal order and economic security.[265]

Changing the Definition of Sin

Some defenders of homosexuality charge that the Old Testament definition does not apply today, that modern homosexuality is not a perversion. Rather, they say, it is an *inversion* of gender identity. Perversion would be considered a person who steps outside their "normal" sexual orientation to pursue the one that is unnatural to them. Inversion, on the other hand, is a supposedly *innocent* mental state of preferring a same-sex relationship over one with the opposite gender. Many would simply say we were just *born* that way. No matter what physical or mental causes are at the heart of "inverted" sexual desires, no blame can or should be assessed by religious moralists against their condition. So say the modern defenders of homosexuality, such as Catholic theologian John J. McNeill, SJ.[266] That author begins with the biblical accounts, then proceeds to tear them down with modern "expert" opinions. McNeill says,

> Finally, we must consider the enormous amount of new, significant data derived from the human sciences such as psychology, psychiatry, sociology, anthropology, and comparative cultural

---

[265] Deuteronomy 28:15ff.
[266] McNeill, *The Church and the Homosexual.*

studies… This data…calls into question many of
the implicit assumptions of the past.[267]

But if this new material has humanism as its starting point—its
worldview—then it is already approaching the area of sexual morality
from the wrong point of view. God had a purpose for human sexuality that remains unchanged going all the way back to creation.
Any view of human sexuality that removes God's covenant relationship with believers as its base is invalid. Science, by definition, makes
observations about *physical* relationships. Since purpose behind
human sexuality is metaphysical—that is, beyond the senses—it is
outside the realm of science, especially the "human" sciences. Here's
another example of McNeill's humanistic thinking:

> Under the influence of recent psychological
> insights there has been a movement away from
> the *act-centered methodology* of the past toward
> an orientation-centered methodology… [T]he
> moral quality of sexual activity cannot be judged
> from the isolated act.[268]

McNeil has this exactly wrong. It is the homosexual *act* that
pointed toward a person's sinful, disordered thinking, and it was the
act that God condemned and punished in the Old Testament. God
did not differentiate between the mental states of the accused homosexual, allowing the one acting from inversion to go free but condemning the act stemming from "perversion." There were no exceptions to
that law in Leviticus 18:22 given to Moses. McNeil states that there is
some "moral quality" to a homosexual act that can't be judged as sin
just by looking at the act itself. This is a serious affront to the holiness
of God and a misunderstanding of the importance of symbolism in
God's mind. The homosexual act, in God's mind, is *always* sin because
it destroys the symbolism that God created opposite-gender marriage

---

[267] McNeill, 19.
[268] McNeill, 18, emphasis mine.

to be. There is no need to wait for a psychological evaluation of that sin before it can be called "sin." This is a direct, frontal attack on the Scriptures as received from God, and yet McNeill chides the "moralists" for not making a distinction between the mental condition of the homosexual and the actual act of homosexuality:

> Many people have had homosexual experiences who do not have a predominantly homosexual *orientation* but are definitely heterosexually inclined. Consequently, it is important *for the moralist* to keep the distinction between homosexual activity and the homosexual condition clearly in mind. For there is an important difference in the moral judgment to be passed on a heterosexual indulging in homosexual activity and a true homosexual indulging in the same behavior as an expression of his or her love.[269]

What McNeill means here is that if you take the Bible literally, you can't judge a homosexual act until you get inside the head of the offender. If that person truly *loves* his partner, this is the "homosexual condition," which is perfectly fine. After all, who can find fault with love?

But surely the heterosexual who is merely indulging his lust should bear the consequence of his sin. As stated earlier, the danger of basing judgments on emotion is that emotions and feelings are never wrong. But God did not pronounce punishment based on our thoughts. He pronounced punishment to those under Mosaic law where someone was caught in the *act* of homosexuality, and then, only if there are two or three witnesses.[270] No one was to be put to death on the word of only one witness. God does not want us to become thought police. But if someone's homosexual thoughts become homosexual *actions*, then that person is guilty of breaking

---

[269] McNeill, 40, emphasis mine.
[270] Deuteronomy 17:6.

God's moral code, whether he loves his partner or not. Furthermore, the only marriage God defines is between a man and a woman. There is no allowance for homosexual "marriage," and so any sexual activity between two same-sex partners is considered sin by God, regardless of any "love" between the parties. "Love" does not justify sex outside marriage in any way whatever. Of course, in the New Testament, indulging in homosexual thoughts are condemned just as much as the act itself.[271]

As confessed homosexuals have increased in numbers and political power (in the West), many Christians have adjusted and even come to full acceptance of the "homosexual condition." Those who accept the theory of inversion over perversion go so far as to say that inversion was never even conceived of by biblical writers such as Moses, Jesus or Paul. The biblical facts are certainly at odds with that position. God never made a distinction between perversion and inversion because there was no distinction to be made. The very act of one man lying sexually with another man was, and is for all time, an abomination to God, who made man and woman in his image at Creation. McNeill criticizes those who hold this position by presenting them with the inhumane treatment that must be suffered by those afflicted by homosexuality. He says,

> The homosexual…must see himself *condemned through no fault of his own* to a life in which every expression of human sexual love will only serve to deepen the hold of an objectively sinful condition on himself and his loved one, separating them further from God's plan. In contradiction to the biblical message that it is by love that one unites oneself to God, the homosexual must see his deepest and most sincere human love as cutting him and his loved one off from God.[272]

---

[271] Matthew 5:27–28 (by applying the regulation against heterosexual lust to homosexual lust).

[272] McNeill. 32, emphasis mine.

First, no one is cut off from the love of God unless they so choose. The biblically-minded Christian certainly empathizes with the condition the homosexual finds himself in. At the same time believers must continue to see that the confusion caused by sin comes from the enemy of God. We must see also that God's prescription for someone so caught in sin is to confess it and then make every possible effort to live by the power of the Holy Spirit moment-by-moment, following the guidance and strength he provides those who love him. We live by God's promise spoken through St. Paul: "So I say, live by the Spirit, and you will not gratify the desires of the sinful nature" (Galatians 5:16). There is a way through the morass of twisted, immoral thinking, a way given by God himself. Those who seek it with all their hearts will find it.

When McNeill or any other counselor claims to speak in God's name and yet uses the human suffering caused by our sin to accept the condition that results from it, using human philosophy and psychiatry to redefine both the sin and the resulting condition into something that Christians are supposed to accept as righteous suffering, such a person is not speaking *for* God. Of *course,* there is suffering involved in this sin. Of *course,* we all have friends or family touched by this disorder. Of *course,* true Christians must deal in great love and understanding with anyone afflicted by these sinful desires and in a way that draws them closer to God rather than pushing them away. But telling people caught up in the sin of homosexuality that they are innocent victims and therefore justified in pursuing their heartfelt desires like any other person is a direct contradiction of Scripture and of God's will for that person.

What We Learn from Opposite-Gender Relationships

In real life, it takes serious effort to understand and learn to live with the peculiarities of the opposite sex. But rejecting the part each partner is to play by seeking a same-sex relationship isn't fulfilling the purpose God had for opposite-gender marriage. There are many things that God desires the male to learn from an opposite-gender committed relationship. One is for the man to take full responsibility for leading and protecting his own family. This is what God does for all believers.

Another thing will probably draw a smile from the average husband. Sometimes—only sometimes—a woman will do something that seems to defy all (male) logic. Those are times when a man must remember that women won't always agree with what seems to men like a perfectly logical position about some domestic matter or other. When you think your wife is driving you crazy, remember this: In your relationship to God, you often drive *him* crazy. Something that seems like a no-brainer and perfectly logical to God—e.g., *Why don't you run away from that sin?*—is something that we, as sinful men, pursue without giving it a second thought. We can plunge headlong into sin and pretend God doesn't see it or doesn't care. In other words, what our wives sometimes do to us, *symbolically*, is similar to what we often do to God in the actual reality of our relationship with him. Understanding your wife symbolically will greatly help your understanding both of God and your wife.

What God wants for the married woman is that she remains loving and faithful while submitting to her own husband, just as all believers must submit to God. (On that point, God is not a slave driver—neither should the husband be). God didn't intend marriage to be easy. He intended it to be a training ground where we can see the effort *he* makes to supply our needs as we seek a relationship with him in *his* world, on *his* terms. The more we understand human marriage and the differences between genders, the more we will come to know how God thinks.

16

Symbolism of the Lamb

I believe in God the Father Almighty, Maker of heaven and earth.

And in Jesus Christ, His only Son, our Lord who...

Suffered under Pontius Pilate; Was crucified, dead and buried.

—Apostles' Creed

I f you grew up in a Christian church, you are probably familiar with the Apostles' Creed, which outlines Jesus' life, his death on the cross, his resurrection from the dead, and other events that followed. We tend to take for granted the fact that Jesus came to earth to be crucified for our sins. Everyone who fully understands their sinful condition is amazed and eternally grateful to God for his love in giving his Son as our way back to the Father, the Creator of our souls. We also hurt over the fact that the first ones Jesus came to rescue were those of the Jewish nation.

Jesus's coming was in fulfillment of all the predictions of the Law and the Prophets. But the prophets also predicted the Messiah would be rejected by his own people, a fact the prophets and Jewish leaders had a hard time reconciling with the victorious resurrection from the dead[273] and the glories that would follow. The average Jewish person in Jesus's day never expected that the Messiah would die on a cross. In fact, dying on the cross may be the single biggest factor that caused Jews to *reject* Jesus as their Messiah, even to this day. By all indications, the prophets foretold that the Messiah would die as an innocent substitute for sin. In the Jewish Bible, God provided at least three historical events of an innocent sacrifice that symbolized the Messiah's death. Along with these symbols, the words of Isaiah predicted the Messiah would be like a lamb led to the slaughter which, over time, formed an expectation in the Jewish mind of what the Messiah would come to do.

Most Israelites would have been familiar with the symbolism of the sacrifice lamb. Those who were not were sure to find out after all the excitement surrounding the ministry of John the Baptist. At the first sign of Jesus, John cried out, "Look! The Lamb of God who takes away the sin of the world!"[274] This cry was what many in Israel had been earnestly waiting for. What they were probably *not* waiting for was the Messiah's being crucified by the Romans, since no sacrifice to God was to be hung on a tree or crucified. Instead, the Jews were looking for victory *over* the Romans. Still, if Jesus were to be the true Messiah, he would have to be put to death as the innocent lamb spoken of by the prophets, in order to pay for the sins of the world. That made Jesus the Messiah the most important fulfillment of symbolism ever devised by God the Father and, like any other symbolism, the meaning and purpose of the symbol was not to be broken, especially not by crucifying the Messiah.

The Jewish View of Crucifixion

The crucifixion of Jesus was considered by contemporaries and by later Jews as the reason he could *not* be the Messiah. In his *Life and Times of Jesus the Messiah*, Alfred Edersheim described Nicodemus

---

[273] Psalm 16:10; see also Hosea 6:1, 2.
[274] John 1:29.

and his view of the cross as being, "the greatest offence to his Jewish thinking."[275] As D. A. Fiensy explained,

> Jews treated the idea of a crucified man of God with great suspicion, since Deut 21:23 pronounced a curse on anyone who was "hanged on a tree."[276]

That curse was clearly stated:

> If a man guilty of a capital offense is put to death and his body is hung on a tree, you must not leave his body on the tree overnight. Be sure to bury him that same day, because anyone who is hung on a tree is under God's curse (Deuteronomy 21:23).

A Jew who looked at this verse could not accept Jesus as their Messiah for two reasons. First, the verse concerned someone "guilty of a capital offense." This simply couldn't apply to the Messiah. Second, it says "anyone hung on a tree is under God's curse." No sacrificial animal was ever hung on a tree. Therefore, neither could Messiah be hung on a tree since he was the fulfillment of that sacrificial lamb symbolism. Since Jesus was hung on a wooden cross, he would certainly be thought of as under God's curse and therefore disqualified from fulfilling the role of unblemished sacrifice.

Animals brought to the temple for sacrifice had to be perfect, without blemish. When discussing Levitical animal sacrifices in the Mosaic law, the term "without defect" is used no less than thirty times. Here are just a few passages that highlight the importance of offering a perfect sacrifice to God:

- "They [the imperfect offerings] will not be accepted on your behalf, because they are deformed and have defects." (Leviticus 22:25)

---

[275] Edersheim, *The Life and Times of Jesus the Messiah*, ch. 6.
[276] Fiensy, *Crucifixion*, in Barry et al. (eds.), *The Lexham Bible Dictionary*.

- "Be sure the animals are without defect." (Numbers 28:31)
- "If an animal has a defect, is lame or blind, or has *any serious flaw*, you must not sacrifice it to the LORD your God." (Deuteronomy 15:21)
- "Do not sacrifice to the LORD your God an ox or a sheep that has any defect *or flaw in it*, for *that would be detestable to him*." (Deuteronomy 17:1)

The Lord Jesus would also have to be without the blemish of sin, so he could be an acceptable sacrifice to the Father. Crucifixion on a Roman cross would have been simply incompatible with the idea of an unblemished sacrifice.

How Later Jews Saw the Crucified Messiah

In second-century AD, Justin Martyr (110–165 AD) wrote a treatise called the *Dialog of Justin with Trypho*. The title of chapter 89 was "The Cross Alone Is offensive to Trypho on Account of the Curse, yet It Proves That Jesus Is Christ." This shows an example of the attitude that many Jews continued to have after the Lord was crucified. Trypho reasoned that since Jesus was crucified (i.e., hung on a tree), this disqualified him from being the Messiah. Trypho began his comments thus:

> Be assured that all our nation waits for Christ; and we admit that all the Scriptures which you have quoted refer to Him. Moreover, I do also admit that the name of Jesus, by which the son of Nave (Nun) was called, has inclined me very strongly to adopt this view. *But whether Christ should be so shamefully crucified, this we are in doubt about.* For whosoever is crucified is said in the law to be accursed, so that I am exceedingly incredulous on this point. It is quite clear, indeed, that the Scriptures announce that Christ had to

suffer; but *we wish to learn if you can prove it to us whether it was by the suffering cursed in the law.*[277]

Clearly, though Trypho was probably a composite character—several of Justin's experiences rolled into one literary character—Trypho nevertheless expressed a view that was most likely common in the first and second centuries and beyond.[278] The Jews acknowledged that Messiah had to suffer but were unwilling to admit without further evidence that the Messiah had to suffer the shame of crucifixion. Trypho continued,

> For we know that He should suffer and be led as a sheep. But prove to us whether He must be crucified and die so disgracefully and so dishonourably by the death cursed in the law. For we cannot bring ourselves even to think of this.[279]

The idea that the Messiah had to die by the humiliation of crucifixion was unthinkable to the Jewish mind. Other non-Christian second-century figures held the same contempt for the crucifixion of the Lord Jesus. Origen, in his *Against Celsus*, noted that Celsus mocked anyone who believed in Jesus because, "he was shamefully bound, and disgracefully punished, and very recently was most contumeliously treated before the eyes of all men."[280]

The well-known ancient author and speaker Cicero (107–47 BC) also recorded his repulsion to this method of torture. According to Cicero, crucifixion was the "most cruel and repulsive punishment."[281] Josephus, in his *Jewish Wars*, said crucifixion was "the most pitiable of deaths."[282] Finally, D. A. Fiensy wrote, "In crucifixion,

---

[277] Justin Martyr, *Dialogue of Justin with Trypho, a Jew*, emphasis mine.

[278] Fiensy, op cit.

[279] Justin Martyr, ibid., ch. 90.

[280] Origen, "Against Celsus," 6.10, Roberts, Donaldson, and Coxe (eds.), *Fathers of the Third Century*.

[281] Cicero, *in Verrem*, 2.5.165, retrieved September 9, 2018.

[282] Jewish Wars, 7.203.

everything was done to humiliate and dishonor the victim in addition to torturing him or her to death."[283]

The Apostle Paul seems to be aware that his contemporaries also believed it was folly to think of the Messiah as crucified when he stated in 1 Corinthians 1:18:

> "For the message of the cross is foolishness to those who are perishing, but to us who are being saved it is the power of God."

In light of Deuteronomy 21:23, it made no sense to the average Jew to believe that God would allow the Messiah to be humiliated and cursed by hanging him on a cross. Crucifixion was simply not the prescribed method of sacrificing the Messiah. God, through three prophetic symbols, revealed what God actually had in mind, because symbolism is how God thinks.

Three Messianic Symbols

Three important symbolic events, all having similar elements, painted a fairly clear picture of what God the Father had in mind for the death of his Son. All these accounts featured a type or symbol of the Messiah, such as a lamb (or, in Isaac's case, Isaac himself as the lamb) and some sort of altar.

The first and greatest symbol, as discussed earlier, was the Sacrifice of Isaac by his father, Abraham. This historic event played out about six hundred years before Israel's exodus out of Egypt. While Abraham and Isaac walked toward the place where the altar was to be built, Isaac asked his father, "Where is the lamb for the burnt offering?" The altar and the lamb are pointed to, but we also see the human father offering his son in a clear display of what God the Father would do in the future to his only Son, Jesus. It is interesting that God provided a ram as the substitute for Isaac. It is Isaac, however, not the ram, who gets the headline in this story. The primary

---

[283] Barry et al., eds., *op cit.*

symbol presented here is the father sacrificing his son, as God commanded. Abraham sacrificing the ram highlights the substitutionary aspect in that God would accept a substitution for his Son until the time chosen by the Father.

In the second significant event foreshadowing the Lord's death, God was about to kill every firstborn son in the kingdom of Egypt. This was God's last judgment against Pharaoh, who was being punished for not letting the Israelites go out to the wilderness to sacrifice to Jehovah. Among the Israelites, God would spare *their* firstborn sons by accepting the life of a lamb in their place. The blood of that lamb was to be smeared on each doorpost of every Jewish household. If the blood were found on the doorpost, that family would be spared the death of their firstborn child and the firstborn from their animals. The doorpost, therefore, became a kind of altar for each Jewish family, with the blood of the lamb smeared upon it. In fact, the word *altar* (Heb. *mizbeakh*) means "any construction of various designs, for the placing of gifts or sacrifices in a ritual to deity."[284] While not an altar in the usual sense, the doorpost served its purpose and was accessible to every Jewish family. The blood on the makeshift altar provided protection from God's wrath for the household. Again, we have both a kind of altar on which the blood of the sacrifice was to be applied, and the sacrifice lamb portraying the sinless, firstborn Son of God, the sole means of protection from God's judgment.

The third important symbol describing the death of the Messiah was the system of animal sacrifice instituted under Moses. When Israel camped at Mount Sinai, God laid out an entire system of laws for Israel to follow regarding the slaughter of innocent animals and applying their blood on an altar especially designed by God for the purpose. Sometimes bulls, goats, or other animals were sacrificed by the person bringing the offering as a covering for his own sin. The symbolism showed just how serious a matter sin was in God's mind, one that could only be covered by the violent death and the shedding of the blood of an innocent substitute—in this case, an animal—and that was only a temporary covering for sin until the promised

---

[284] Swanson, *Dictionary of Biblical Languages with Semantic Domains, mizbeakh.*

Messiah would make the atonement for sin permanent. The shedding of blood was significant because, as Leviticus 17:11 states,

> The life of a creature is in the blood, and I have
> given it to you to make atonement for yourselves
> on the altar; it is the blood that makes atonement
> for one's life.

The violent death of the sacrifice was intended as a substitute for the person offering it. However, there was another animal, a male lamb, which was the first offering of the day, and another male lamb which was the last offering of the day.[285] These were to be burnt offerings, offered each day for all the generations to come. These possibly symbolized the Messiah who went before and after every other offering of each day, the Alpha and the Omega,[286] and the First and the Last,[287] since God was foreshadowing a violent death for his Son, the Lord Jesus Christ, as well. With his death, forgiveness of sins would become permanent for all who believe and the beginning of the end of Satan's rule on the earth. It is important to note that, once again, the altar and the lamb were a prominent part of the Levitical sacrificial system.

In each of those three prophetic events, God gave very specific instructions to be carried out in a way for their symbolism to be pleasing to God. The ceremonies were to be carefully observed so that when Messiah arrived, there would be no mistaking what he came to do.

Despite the detailed instructions given by God for the symbolic events, the actual future sacrifice of the Messiah had no specific instructions laid down by God. Only the broad strokes of his ceremonial death were foreshadowed. Given the seriousness of symbolism to God, it would have made sense for the Lamb of God to offer his life at the altar of the temple in Jerusalem, more so since the Temple

---

285 Exodus 29:38, 39.
286 Revelation 1:8.
287 Revelation 1:17.

Mount happened to be on the very same spot where Abraham had almost sacrificed Isaac. There was just one small problem. In places like Isaiah 53, God foresaw that the Jewish leaders would reject and brutalize the Messiah. That would seem to make him a blemished sacrifice and therefore unfit to serve as the Messiah. The symbolism that would have satisfied God's desire to bring forgiveness and atonement for the sins of the world would be rejected by those whom the Messiah came to save. Perhaps this is why the method and circumstances of putting Messiah to death were purposely left open, leaving it up to the rulers of Israel to ultimately decide Messiah's fate, depending on whether or not they received him as their King and hailed Jesus as Israel's Sacrifice Lamb, or put him to a shameful death as an imposter.

Stepping into the Unknown

For those who lived *prior* to Jesus' birth (and who would include Satan and his demon army), a *literal* interpretation of Levitical symbolism would seem to require that Messiah offer himself *on the altar at the Jerusalem temple*, and by now we all know how God the Father feels about the literal fulfillment of symbolism. Offering himself on that special altar, and having the High Priest apply his blood to the mercy seat behind the curtain leading to the most holy place, would be the most sensible way and the greatest, most complete way of fulfilling the Mosaic law. It was also the very reason the Lord Jesus took upon himself a human body. Consider this messianic passage from the book of Hebrews, quoting from Psalm 40:

> Sacrifice and offering you did not desire,
> but a body you prepared for me;
> With burnt offerings and sin offerings
> you were not pleased.
> Then I said,
> "Here I am—it is written about me in the scroll—

I have come to do your will, O God." [288]

In this prophecy the Son of God before coming to earth, was volunteering himself in place of the animal sacrifices (which never fully satisfied God the Father), and he was offering to do so with excitement in his voice. "Here I am!" he said. This is exactly what symbolism is: one thing standing for another. The Lord Jesus was willing to take on human flesh and step into the unknown, into the world that Satan ruled, and have his blood shed in order to please the Father and do his will. It is both wonderful and horrible to ponder the idea that Jesus, while still in heaven before coming to earth, would have known these two things by his divine foreknowledge— first, that his ministry would end being scourged and nailed to a Roman cross, and second, that he would still unhesitatingly volunteer himself to the Father to face that horrible death as seen in Psalm 40 above.

As if that weren't enough, when the Son of God left heaven to take on human flesh, he would set aside all foreknowledge of his ultimate fate on the cross in order to take on the limits of a human body. His earliest thoughts would not include any knowledge of his fateful death on the cross. He would, in effect, be a blank slate as far as future events were concerned, until such time as the Father saw fit to reveal that knowledge to him sometime during his ministry—possibly as late as the Mount of Transfiguration, about a year before his death.[289] However, even without special revelation from the Father, he would have known from ancient prophecies that he would die some kind of violent death, knowing that all sacrifices to God in the temple required such a death for the animal and that it would be no different for him. It was, in fact, the violent aspect of the death of a sacrifice that assuaged the anger that God held against the rebellion of sin.

The Lord Jesus himself, during his ministry, practically invited the Pharisees to threaten him with death for breaking the sabbath

---

[288] Hebrews 10:5–7; Psalm 40:6-8, Septuagint
[289] Cheney, *Jesus Christ*, 138.

laws. On one such occasion, the disciples were picking heads of grain on the sabbath. Though the Lord himself was not taking any of the grain, teachers of the law believed that leaders could be held liable for their followers' actions.[290] The Pharisees said to Jesus, "Look, why are they doing what is unlawful[291] on the sabbath?" The phrase *what is unlawful* was a Pharisaic formula[292] used as a warning to point out to Jesus that the disciples were violating a law that could lead to prosecution. Such a warning was required by Jewish law to be given prior to pursuing any legal charge of breaking the sabbath, an offense that carried the death penalty.[293] The Lord Jesus would have recognized the threat immediately. Yet he was never dissuaded from pursing truth even if it meant surrendering his life in the service of making God's loving heart known to those who had long forgotten how to serve him. Without his powers of foreknowledge, the Lord Jesus placed himself at a severe disadvantage as far as his human flesh is concerned, but with his divine nature guiding his human spirit and his daily, deep prayer life, he was always led by the Holy Spirit, and therefore able to receive and follow every command given him by the Father even if it led to dangerous encounters with his enemies.

Punishment for Broken Symbolism

Though the symbolism of the Messiah dying on the altar as an unblemished sacrifice was never carried out, God the Father allowed the Lord Jesus to be cursed in our place by having him hung on a wooden cross, the "tree" of Deuteronomy 21. With his death, the symbolism of the sacrifice lamb was lost, at a great cost to Israel. The Lord Jesus alluded to this lost symbolism during the Triumphal Entry where he addressed those who rejected him:

---

[290] Lane, *The Gospel of Mark*; Mark 2:23–24, Logos electronic edition.

[291] Gk., "*ho ouk exestin*," or "what is unlawful."

[292] Foerster, ἔξεστιν, ἐξουσία, ἐξουσιάζω, κατεξουσιάζω; Kittel, Bromiley, and Friedrich (eds.), *Theological dictionary of the New Testament*, 560–575.

[293] Lane, citing M. Sanhedrin VII. 8.

As he approached Jerusalem and saw the city, he wept over it and said, "If you, even you, had only known on this day *what would bring you peace—* but now it is hidden from your eyes. The days will come upon you when your enemies will build an embankment against you and encircle you and hem you in on every side. They will dash you to the ground, you and the children within your walls. They will not leave one stone on another, *because you did not recognize* the time of God's coming to you."[294]

In the words "If you, even you, had only known on this day what would bring you peace," you can almost hear Jesus's thoughts trail off into another reality where he would have been received as Messiah. What did he mean by "what would bring you peace"? What *would* have brought Israel peace at this time? Peace would have come if Israel had recognized God was visiting them in the person of the long-awaited Messiah. And what was it that Messiah was going to come and do, but "give himself a ransom for many?"[295] But now, as he said, this was hidden from the eyes of those who should have seen it coming. Jesus then tied this blindness to a coming punishment resulting from his rejection.

All Jerusalem would be destroyed as useless, since she failed at her paramount "reason for being"—to recognize what fulfilled messianic symbolism should have looked like and then to believe John the Baptist's testimony and receive Jesus of Nazareth as her Messiah. The Romans would not "leave one stone on another, because you did not recognize the time of God's coming to you."[296] Even though the Lord knew, toward the end, that his final breath would be from the cross and not the altar, he faithfully proceeded with his ministry and fulfillment of prophecies as though nothing stood in his way. He would force the Jewish leadership to block his way to the altar. The greatest

---

[294] Luke 19:41–44.
[295] Matthew 20:28.
[296] Luke 19:44.

of God's symbols throughout the ages would be shattered—the sacrifice of the Lamb of God at the altar of the temple—and Israel would have a horrible price to pay for it.

One Last Request, Denied

If we fast-forward to the garden of Gethsemane, just before Jesus is taken away for trial, there is *still* indication that the Lord Jesus was desirous of avoiding the cross and going to the altar instead. During his three, deeply emotional and urgent prayers in the garden he prayed, "*Abba*, Father, everything is possible for you. Take this cup from me. Yet not what I will, but what you will."[297] "And there appeared to him an angel from heaven, strengthening him."[298] What other option could there have been than going to the altar instead of the inevitable torture of flogging and crucifixion? Having his neck pierced by a razor-sharp blade at the altar would have felt like a merciful pinprick by comparison. This was not, mind you, a prayer to avoid his sacrifice altogether. Just a few days before he had said,

> Now my heart is troubled, and what shall I say?
> "Father, save me from this hour"? No, it was for
> this very reason I came to this hour. Father, glo-
> rify your name![299]

He went back a second time and prayed, "My Father, if it is not possible for this cup to be taken away unless I drink it, may your will be done."[300] After finding the disciples asleep again, he prayed yet a third time.[301] Offering himself at the altar would have been a greater fulfillment of symbolism and would have spared the Lord much unnecessary pain. But that was not the Father's way. From the parables, we see that when the Master prepared a banquet but

---

[297] Mark 14:36.
[298] Luke 22:43.
[299] John 12:27–28.
[300] Mark 14:39.
[301] Mark 14:41; Lane, *The Gospel of Mark*, Mark 14:39–40.

those who were invited did not come, the Master did not force them to come. Instead, he went out to the roads and country lanes and invited anyone who wanted to celebrate with the Master.[302] God does not suffer insult easily. If the Jews would not come, he would go to the Gentiles. So with the strength of the Father and the Spirit, the Lord Jesus obeyed the Father's will by going to the cross.

Since God thinks in symbols, the will of the Father would have been more perfectly fulfilled if Jewish leaders had accepted Jesus as Messiah and let him offer himself as a sacrifice at the altar of the Jerusalem temple. This would have prevented the later defense by the Jews that no one claiming to be Messiah would have suffered the shame and curse of being hung on (or nailed to) a tree as Jesus was. But this didn't prevent the Father from finding an alternate path by which he would be satisfied with the death of his Son, even though it was by allowing him to be hung from a tree, causing him to fall under God's curse. The Apostle Paul stated in Galatians 3:13,

> Christ redeemed us from the curse of the law by becoming a curse for us, for it is written: "Cursed is everyone who is hung on a tree." [14] He redeemed us in order that the blessing given to Abraham might come to the Gentiles through Christ Jesus, so that by faith we might receive the promise of the Spirit.

Paul explained that the way to look at the crucifixion of Jesus was not that he became the long-awaited sacrificial lamb offered on the altar for our sin. Instead, Paul emphasized that we were cursed for breaking the law but the Lord Jesus became a curse for us when he was hung on the cross. If Satan were pushing for Jesus to go to the cross, knowing that such a death would invalidate Jesus's claim of being a perfect sacrifice, then Satan made a great miscalculation. God took the broken symbolism that focused on Messiah's payment for sin and reengineered it. Instead of its being the sacrifice Lamb, God

---

[302] Luke 14:16–24.

turned the cross into a symbol of Messiah taking onto himself the curse that was on humanity for breaking the Law. The cross became a makeshift altar. It is very interesting that, while Paul picked up on the change in metaphor, Peter chose not to do so. Peter wrote:

> For you know that it was not with perishable things such as silver or gold that you were redeemed…but with the precious blood of Christ, *a lamb without blemish or defect*. He was chosen before the creation of the world but was revealed in these last times for your sake.[303]

As Apostle to the Jews, Peter likely found it more suitable to his audience to keep the sacrifice lamb metaphor when he wrote. Technically, Peter was still correct. Jesus lived his entire life without blemish or defect. Paul did not invalidate the idea that Jesus was the Sacrifice Lamb of God, but he did change the metaphor, laying more emphasis on Jesus being a curse for us than on his being the Sacrifice Lamb. It was the unjust condemnation of Jesus by the Jewish leaders and being hung on the cross that brought cursing from the Father. God changed the messianic symbol from dying honorably at the altar to dying a dishonorable death, taking on the curse that should have fallen on each human being. Satan must have been furious that God so changed the meaning of the messianic symbolism.

---

[303] 1 Peter 1:18–20, emphasis mine.

17

Broken Symbolism and Final Judgment

We give thanks to you, Lord God Almighty…
  because you have taken your great power
  and have begun to reign…
The time has come for…
  rewarding your servants the prophets
  and your saints
  and those who reverence your name…
And for destroying those who destroy the earth.

—the twenty-four elders
seated before the throne of God
Revelation 11:17–18

Now that the greatest symbolism of all the ages has been broken and rejected by Jews and Gentiles alike, what is left for civilization except eventual judgment and ultimate destruction? After giving his life in the way ordained by the Father, as a cursed sacrifice on the cross, Jesus took his blood to the temple in heaven and applied it to the mercy seat, on top of the ark of the covenant. This, at least, fulfilled the heavenly part of messianic symbolism that the leaders of Israel prevented from being fulfilled in the earthly temple. Jesus then sat down at the right hand of God awaiting the great judgments to come at the end of the age. And come they will.

Christ's Victory, Satan's Revenge

As it now stands, Satan is furious with God and the nation of Israel, who brought forth the Messiah despite Jesus's rejection by the Jewish leadership. The Apostle John, in Revelation 12, relates a vision he saw in heaven which tells of Satan's fury and what he is busy doing right now. It is entirely possible that Satan was furious because he thought he was victorious over Jesus by having him hung on a cross and cursed by God the Father, leaving him disqualified from consideration as an unblemished sacrifice. Instead, God accepted Jesus's sacrifice, and Satan was the one burned.

The vision begins with a woman and a dragon. The woman was about to give birth, and the dragon was in front of her, waiting to snatch the child away from her,[304] an obvious reference to Jesus, and the woman probably a symbolic reference to Israel, the wife of Jehovah, rather than to Mary, the human mother of Jesus. Either way, as soon as the woman gave birth, God the Father snatched the child up to heaven before Satan had half a chance to grab him.[305] This vision is the equivalent of doing a victory dance over an embarrassingly defeated enemy. It leaves the impression that God outmaneuvered Satan so badly that the Lord Jesus was never in any real danger from the Enemy during his entire time on earth. That's how outsmarted Satan was, and now he's furious—at us. John encapsulated what was to happen in the current age in this verse from his vision:

> Then the dragon was enraged at the woman and went off to make war against the rest of her offspring—those who obey God's commandments and hold to the testimony of Jesus.[306]

The "rest of her offspring" is the Church—those who hold fast to their belief in Jesus and his promise to return one day in victory.

---

[304] Revelation 12:2–4.
[305] Revelation 12:5.
[306] v. 17.

Now, Christians in the formerly Christian West are really beginning to feel the heat of Satan's wrath.

Satan's Attack

Satan's method of attack is to get as many as possible to reject God's authority over them and to obliterate the symbolism God designed into creation. He has a multitude of ways to attack the West, a region once undeniably Christian in its worldview and its understanding of biblical morality and symbolism.

First, he has transformed the divine institution of marriage into an unnecessary memory of societies past. What's wrong with the current thinking is that marriage isn't needed to have a consensual sexual relationship. Skipping marriage and going for semicommitted relationships seems a better option than dealing with the turmoil of divorce. Entire generations have become enflamed with sexual liberation, lust, rebellion, perversion, and the standard method of dealing with the consequences of unwanted pregnancy: abortion. The reinterpreted symbolism of sex and marriage goes something like this: "Hey, God created sex for human enjoyment so why limit that to married couples? If sex represents the pleasure of a relationship with God, why not include everybody? Why require a committed relationship? God is love, so he should just let everybody go to heaven, so we can all worship God and have fun together!" This may not be exactly what is going through the mind of every debauched hedonist, but it surely is how God interprets their actions in terms of symbolism.

God absolutely does expect a committed relationship with people before opening up the pleasures of heaven to them. Sexual pleasure should be thought of as God's wedding gift to newly married couples. But today's sexual liberation and the abortion that sometimes follows is a major attack on marital, gender, and sexual symbolism, not to mention an attack on life itself. Other than the sacrificial death of Jesus, marriage was the most important way God demonstrated how much he wants a committed, loving relationship with each person throughout all generations. With the new sexual freedom of the '60s and '70s, homosexuality also erupted from behind closed doors. In all cases, the new morality was an attack on sex that God intended as a symbol of his faithfulness toward mankind. God does not take this attack lightly and Satan knows it.

The End of Patriarchy

As the end of the age nears, human rebellion also extends to the male headship and protection over the home, mirroring Christ's headship over the Church. This and all the other Christian rules are considered "chains" by many feminists. These natural laws were instituted by God and were intended to give us long and prosperous lives. We will see whether the new feminism can redefine patriarchal societies by continuing to weaken leadership roles typically filled by males and pushing masculinity out of the way once and for all. That may cause a vacuum that feminism can't fill or might not want to fill.

As mentioned before, God is half female in his character, perhaps even more than half. The Apostle John wrote, "God is love."[307] Love is what defines him. If the defining characteristics of a woman include love, nurturing, and compassion, then it stands to reason that the woman bears at least as much resemblance to God as the man. Men and women are not the same. They are complimentary; this is just the way God designed us. However, God refers to himself in Scripture in male terms rather than female. God created Adam first and made him head of the family as far back as the garden of Eden. He has also given the leadership role in the church to men rather than women. Perhaps the reason for this is that in this world, where Satan causes so much hostility that leads to conflict, men are less likely to give in to fear and other emotions that may interfere with their decisions.

Regarding our standing before God, men and women are equal—there is no distinction. A woman's relationship to God is no less important than a man's. As Paul said, "There is neither...male nor female, for you are all one in Christ Jesus" (Galatians 3:28). Jesus also said, "At the resurrection people will neither marry nor be given in

---

[307] 1 John 4:8.

marriage; they will be like the angels in heaven."[308] As men and women gain wisdom with age, both have roles to play in society. In the world to come, it will become plain that women represent the deeply emotional nature of God. Their spirit has a valid role to play, every bit as much as a man's less emotional, more cerebral one. Together, man and woman form a complete picture of what God is like. Feminists should take this to heart and be less concerned with overturning God's created order, taking over the roles of both male and female.

Churning Up the Nations

Breaking down borders is another way Satan is defeating the Christian West. In the book of Acts, Paul told the Athenian elders that God

> made every nation of men, that they should inhabit the whole earth; and he determined the times set for them and the exact places where they should live.[309]

God himself set borders between nations and peoples of the earth. God first began to do this back in the time of the Tower of Babel, after the Flood, in order to keep mankind from growing too strong and rebelling against God.[310] In addition to confusing the language common to Noah and his sons, God also divided the land mass into continents. According to Scripture, this happened during the lifetime of Peleg, five generations from Noah, some one hundred to three hundred years after the flood.[311] These barriers are being broken down in record numbers, with millions of immigrants, many from non-Christian worldviews, moving into formerly Christian (or nominally Christian) countries, especially in Europe and the US. This is causing great disturbance in the host countries where Christian

---

[308] Matthew 22:30.
[309] Acts 17:26.
[310] Genesis 11:5–8.
[311] See Genesis 10:25 and Genesis 11:10–19.

and non-Christian worldviews are clashing, often violently, as seen in the Muslim migration into Europe. Satan is surely using this migration to further weaken and break apart the Christian worldview in the West.

Worshiping the Earth

Next, Satan has begun to attack those who are perceived as abusing the natural resources of the planet. Anyone who is seen by the political left as contributing to the worsening of climate change is to be punished, preferably by governments or, failing that, by more direct measures if need be. Satan is fanning the flames of this movement since he knows God will one day take back the earth by force (perhaps sooner rather than later), and that means influencing the earth worshipers to blame the "climate deniers" (which includes many Christians) for the havoc that is coming upon the earth.

God is responsible for the judgments that are coming, in response to the ungodliness of those who refuse to worship God. God is coming "to destroy those who destroy the Earth" (Revelation 11:18). In God's mind, it is the immorality of the ungodly that destroys the earth, not the CO_2 emissions from those guilty of nothing more than breathing the air. The climate change movement may be a sign God has already begun to take back the planet. Satan knows all about the environmental disasters God will eventually level against this rebellious world. It is at least possible Satan himself is gently pushing nonbelievers to lay the blame on those who don't worship the earth as they do. When natural disasters *really* heat up, they will eventually lay the blame squarely on God himself. God's purpose in destroying this beautiful planet is to remove that which the rebellious rely on most: a stable, mostly nonthreatening environment on the planet. Satan will do everything possible to lay environmental disasters at the feet of people who are guilty of nothing more than using the earth's resources, such as fossil fuels, for the purposes God intended.

Since atheism precludes our worship of God, earth worship fills the void. If God did not bring us into being, then we must protect the mechanism that did, and the earth itself (according to nonbelievers) is that mechanism. "We don't need to know where matter came from. It's here, and we're here, and that's all we need to know. And we don't have to rely on any gods to explain how we got here. All that matters now is that we protect the planet. By force if necessary." This is another of Satan's great deceptions and it now produces its share of protectors, including many in the scientific community, condemning and setting out to destroy anything or anyone perceived to be a threat to our planet. Nonbelievers think their existence depends completely on their militant attitude of keeping the environment healthy and trashing any and all climate deniers, especially Christians defending God and traditional morality. "Earth idolatry" is a fitting name for this new faith, and it describes the direction in which Satan is moving the nations of the world, that and an "anything goes" sexual morality. It is idolatry because it substitutes something else for God (in this case, the earth itself), and therefore, this, too, is seen by God as broken symbolism.

Destruction of the Earth

God will, in fact, completely destroy the earth as Peter wrote in 2 Peter 3:7: "The present heavens and earth are reserved for fire, being kept for the day of judgment and destruction of ungodly men." God will rebuild it later into something that cannot be destroyed.[312] No doubt it will pain the Lord to destroy the beautiful things he created, but taking away those things that make nonbelievers feel secure will be a convincing way to bring some to repentance, though not all. Just before the Second Coming, a period known as the Day of the Lord, begins. It is a time of horrible tribulation on the earth, followed by the Second Coming and the millennium, that thousand-year reign of Christ upon the earth, at least according to many Bible expositors. The book of Zephaniah and other passages detail this period of judgments that is also described in Revelation. The opening verses give this warning:

---

[312] 2 Peter 3:13; Revelation 21.

"I will sweep away everything from the face of
the earth,"
declares the LORD.
"I will sweep away both men and animals;
I will sweep away the birds of the air and the fish
of the sea.
The wicked will have only heaps of rubble
when I cut off man from the face of the earth,"
declares the LORD.[313]

The Apostle John listed many things in the book of Revelation
that will occur during that Day of the Lord, initially destroying many
people and much of the environment. Jesus said that precursors to
the Day of the Lord will come upon the earth slowly, like a woman in
childbirth.[314] At first, some bad things we already experience will be
intensified, such as wars, famine, murders, plagues, and even death
by wild animal attacks.[315] This destruction will be set in motion by
the four horsemen of the Apocalypse.[316] They are mobilized when
Jesus breaks the first four of seven wax seals on the scroll of God, the
title deed to planet Earth. The next two seals are other judgments
including the martyrdom of many Christians plus disruptions and
signs in the sky. These judgments constitute the first six seals that
the Lord Jesus himself will peel off the scroll of God which shows his
ownership of the earth and his right to take it back from Satan.

Again, a keen observer might say the intensification of these
signs has already begun. For example, the second horseman was
"given a large sword" and "power to take peace from the earth and to
make men slay each other."[317] This could very well explain the rash
in past years of people randomly shooting, terrorizing, and killing
each other. If so, this is further evidence that God has already started
bringing earth, as we know it, to a close. No specific period is associ-

---

[313] Zephaniah 1:2, 3.
[314] 1 Thessalonians 5:3, Matthew 24:8
[315] Revelation 6:8
[316] Revelation 6
[317] Revelation 6:3-4

ated with these "beginning of birth pains" so no attempt at setting a date for Jesus's return is attempted here.

The Apostle Paul wrote in Romans 8 that the earth itself was already reeling, not from climate change, but from the sins of mankind which are committed against God.[318] He was referring to his own time, all the way back in first-century AD, but things are steadily worsening in our day.

The seventh seal in Revelation 8 brings with it seven trumpet judgments, four of which attack the environment, the greatest possession the nonbeliever has, after his or her own body. First, a third of the land will be burned up and all the green grass. Next a third of all the sea creatures will be killed, followed by a third of all the fresh water on earth ruined. After this, a third of the stars will go dark. These events are the climate worshipers' worst nightmare. What they don't know is that these things are coming no matter how much CO_2 we stop producing and no matter whether the earth heats up or cools down. This is God's direct attack on people who depend upon (and therefore idolize) earthly things rather than depending on and worshiping him. Other judgments will continue to be poured out on earth, but God will not forget about those who love him. They have the promise of God's protection. Opinions vary on whom this promise is addressed to, and whether they are taken out of the earth or are protected from what is happening while still on the earth, but it certainly refers to believers in Jesus. God said in Revelation 3:10,

> Since you have kept my command to endure patiently, I will also keep you from the hour of trial that is going to come upon the whole world to test those who live on the earth.

The Greek words for *keep you from* are the words *tereo ek,* which also appear in John 17:15 and are translated there as *protect from.* Somehow, God's protective hand will be on those believers who are alive at this time.

---

[318] Romans 8:22

Signs of the Times

Satan's attacks are already clearly seen. By the time God is ready to wrap up human history at the end of the age, most people on earth will have followed the various deceptions of Satan and turned away from the salvation offered by our loving Creator. That time seems to be upon us now and Satan seems to be showing more of his fury with each passing year. Due to the darkness in the minds of those who choose not to follow God, the Christian worldview has now been stamped out of most Western schools and universities and out of most political discourse in the public square. All the beautiful symbolism and whatever positive influence Christianity has had on people and nations throughout Western history is slowly but unmistakably vanishing. God's authority is what the Western worldview formerly depended on to keep some semblance of order in society. But with that slowly being swept away, Christians are already struggling to maintain legitimacy in the world against the fiery darts of the Enemy. They are increasingly blamed for the problems in society and the environment that the accusers have actually brought upon themselves.

No Symbolism, No Meaning—Only Darkness

In the book of Romans, Paul outlined the moral death-spiral resulting from the rejection of God's preeminence and authority, as well as from the destruction of the symbolism he has built into Creation. Paul said,

> For although they knew God, they neither glorified him as God nor gave thanks to him, but their thinking became futile and their foolish hearts were darkened.[319]

---

[319] Romans 1:21.

The Greek phrase "their thinking became futile" has the meaning of becoming "useless and hence, worthless" or even becoming "nonsense."[320] One first-century BC philosopher referred to this futility as "the nothingness of man,"[321] similar to Solomon's cry, "Utterly meaningless! Everything is meaningless!"[322] Where humanism reigns—and this was the worldview from which Solomon wrote—all is, ultimately, meaningless, since there is no agreed-upon foundation on which to build truth. The clear conclusion is that a futile life is one devoid of symbolism and therefore meaning, since meaning is the accumulation of important symbols in one's life. It is empty, it is nothingness. This nothingness is exactly why all of us need an authority like God over us. He leads us in the best way to go.

> The mind of sinful man is death, but the mind controlled by the Spirit is life and peace, the sinful mind is hostile to God. It does not submit to God's law, nor can it do so. Those controlled by the sinful nature cannot please God.[323]

One popular saying has it that people are born with a "God-shaped hole" in their hearts. That hole cannot be filled by looking inward since our inner souls are precisely the source of the emptiness. Blaise Pascal, the seventeenth-century French mathematician, inventor, and Catholic theologian, likely authored the idea when he said,

> There was once in man a true happiness, of which all that now remains is the empty print and trace... [T]his infinite abyss can be filled

---

[320] Louw and Nida, *Greek-English Lexicon of the New Testament*; LN65.38, "futile," ματαιόομαι (*mataióomai*).

[321] Philodemus of Gadara (110–28 BC), in Bauernfeind, *Mataios*; Kittel, Bromiley, and Friedrich (eds.), *Theological Dictionary of the New Testament*, 519–524). Grand Rapids.

[322] Ecclesiastes 1:2.

[323] Romans 8:6–8.

only with an infinite and immutable object; in
other words, by God himself.[324]

After Paul described how the nonbeliever's thinking is futile, he
added to it by saying, "Their foolish hearts were darkened."[325] As if
looking inward and finding nothingness wasn't enough, those who
have left God find only darkness when they look outside themselves
as well. The Greek word for darkened[326] is to be understood as the
inability to see the world in any meaningful way rather than simply
referring to any kind of literal darkness. This kind of darkness acts
as "an enveloping sphere," surrounding a person, making him or her
feel "a hindrance to movement and action, to foresight" and giving
the sensation of "objective peril and subjective anxiety."[327] There is no
symbolism in this depth of darkness in the heart of the nonbeliever.
It is simply confusion, brought about by the great author of confusion: Satan. Such people feel like the world is closing in on them. But
instead of reaching out to God, they strike out at anyone or anything
they feel contributes to their fear.

In Psalm 82, Asaph wrote about the impact the evil spirits in God's divine council were having on the world God created.
Almighty God rebuked those lesser "gods," telling them that they
walked around in darkness. This darkness was shaking the very foundations of the earth.

> God presides in the great assembly;
> he gives judgment among the "gods":
> "How long will you defend the unjust
> and show partiality to the wicked?   *Selah*
> Defend the cause of the weak and fatherless;
> maintain the rights of the poor and oppressed.
> Rescue the weak and needy;

---

[324] Pascal, Blaise. *Pensées*, retrieved November 4, 2018.

[325] v. 21.

[326] Gk. "skotidzo."

[327] Conzelmann, σκότος, σκοτία, σκοτόω, σκοτίζω, σκοτεινός; Kittel, Bromiley,
and Friedrich (eds.), *Theological Dictionary of the New Testament* 423–445.

deliver them from the hand of the wicked.
"They know nothing, they understand nothing.
They walk about in darkness;
all the foundations of the earth are shaken.
"I said, 'You are "gods";
you are all sons of the Most High.'
But you will die like mere men;
you will fall like every other ruler."

This darkness originates in the spirit world. When manifested in our world, those who walk in darkness become unable to comprehend the world around them. The anxiety that results from their inner darkness explains why many of today's non-Christians are so irrationally angry. They are angry at those who oppose their rebellion against God. Without the work of the Holy Spirit, those in darkness will not comprehend or accept the symbolism which they are destroying by their actions. When the symbolism behind God's creation is ignored, the thinking of those ignoring him necessarily becomes futile and dark since those rejecting the truth must invent some other subjective, alternative truth that does not fit the pattern of the world around them.

Francis Crick, the famed explorer of the DNA molecule, defended the idea of an alternate truth needed to, in effect, replace God as Creator when he declared, "Biologists must constantly keep in mind that what they see [in DNA and elsewhere] was not designed, but rather, evolved."[328] Crick couldn't have gotten it more wrong. Thankfully, a growing number of scientists admit to the design of DNA by God. To keep one's sanity, we are absolutely required to live our lives as though God really did create the universe. Nonbelievers might deny it, but the universe itself keeps reeling them in like a fish on a hook. Every soul is dark without God's truth. Every nonbeliever must deny God every day by rejecting the authorship of the world around them that reflects every aspect of God's character in symbolic

---

[328] Crick, *What Mad Pursuit: A Personal View of Scientific Discovery*, 20.

form. Truly did David write, "The heavens declare the glory of God, the skies proclaim the work of his hands."[329]

Stamping Out the Christian Worldview

Those who follow *any* path away from God—whether radical environmentalism, scientific materialism, sexual immorality, or radical feminism—the biggest danger in following the path away from God and into darkness is that those who follow it will not rest until they successfully impose their ideas on those who disagree with them. If they fail to gain voluntary compliance, they will try to obtain it by appealing to governments for relief and validation or even certification. This could explain the eventual turn toward martyring Christians in Revelation 6:9 for their stubborn lack of acceptance of the nothingness worldview. They have thrown God, nature, and symbolism out with the trash. Such thinking is worthless in the strongest sense of that word, abandoning any sense of worth to the way they were created by God. Paul states forcefully,

> If our [good news][330] is veiled, it is veiled to those who are perishing. The god of this age has blinded the minds of unbelievers, so that they cannot see the light of the [good news] of the glory of Christ, who is the image of God.[331]

The "god of this age," Satan, is always behind the opinions and arguments that draw God's creatures into darkness and confusion.

Anything But God: Man's Rebellion

The worldwide persecution and martyrdom of Christians is symbolic of Satan's complete takeover of the earth and the repudi-

---

[329] Psalm 19:1.
[330] NIV: "gospel."
[331] 2 Corinthians 4:3–4

ation of Jesus as King over his creation. What horrific, broken symbolism this is. The persecution occurs before and after the Lord Jesus opens the fifth seal on the scroll of God in Revelation 6. At the opening of that seal, God recognizes those who were already martyred and honors them with white robes and a promise that he will visit his vengeance on the killers. There would be many more martyrs to come. The opening of the sixth seal brings a great earthquake, fearsome enough to shake the confidence of the mightiest people on earth. This group of people consists of the "kings of the earth, the princes, the generals, the rich, and the mighty."[332] The sun and moon are also disrupted, mountains are leveled, and the sky appears to be peeled away. This judgment is so harsh that these world leaders will change their minds about the cause of this environmental disaster. They will all realize that no amount of ozone loss or carbon dioxide from human beings could possibly be the cause of what they are witnessing. They will recognize that what they once saw as natural disasters caused by climate change were actually judgments from God. Up until that point, those leaders will have been ruling in open defiance against him. When the earthquake strikes, they will see these disasters as symbolic of God's judgment rather than the result of man's abuse of the planet which (they believed) led to disastrous climate change. After the earthquake, these brave leaders will be turned into fearful little children. They will call out to the mountains and say,

> Fall on us and hide us from the face of him who sits on the throne and from the wrath of the Lamb! For the great day of their wrath has come, and who can stand?[333]

It would be better for them to call out to God and beg for forgiveness, something God would be very willing to grant.

These leaders will draw the same conclusion that the pagan Roman centurion drew after Jesus was put to death on the cross. After Jesus gave

---

[332] v. 15.
[333] vss. 16–17

up his spirit there was an immediate and violent earthquake so strong that the thick curtain in the temple that guarded the Most Holy place was torn in half.[334] This was the most important place on earth to those Jewish leaders who rejected Jesus. At that moment, the centurion directing the crucifixion, and the soldiers with him, said, "Surely, he was the Son of God!"[335] One thing that rulers of the earth understand is power, and power from God is what will be on display at this future time.

While repentance and turning to God for deliverance would seem to be the right move during this destruction, nonbelievers instead will do just the opposite:

> The rest of mankind that were not killed by these plagues still did not repent of the work of their hands; they did not stop worshiping demons, and idols of gold, silver, bronze, stone and wood—idols that cannot see or hear or walk. Nor did they repent of their murders, their magic arts, their sexual immorality or their thefts.[336]

Mankind is in a state of rebellion against God and has been since the Garden.

> The kings of the earth take their stand
> and the rulers gather together against the LORD
> and against his Anointed One.
> "Let us break their chains," they say,
> "and throw off their fetters."
> The One enthroned in heaven laughs;
> the Lord scoffs at them.[337]

---

[334] According to Jewish written tradition, the curtain was as thick as a handbreadth, or about four inches. See https://cbumgardner.wordpress.com/2010/04/06/the-thickness-of-the-temple-veil/. Retrieved January 13, 2019.

[335] Matthew 27:51–54.

[336] Revelation 9:20–21.

[337] Psalm 2:3–4.

The Lord laughs and scoffs at them because they have been deceived into thinking that they have the correct worldview. God knows otherwise.

Judgment of the Symbol Breakers

The destruction God brings about on Judgment Day might be something we would rather not dwell on for long. It seems so incompatible with his loving character, but God is righteous in all his ways despite the terrible times that are coming upon the earth. He is aware of every sentient being's every thought. His awareness extends to eternity past and reaches into eternity future. God is righteous and true in all his judgments.

The meticulous judgment and complete destruction of the current order reflects the depth of God's feelings toward the former perfection of his creation. There are many things we do not know about how God thinks. But God has left us much revelation and teaching about himself over many ages through his prophets. By sending his Son to walk with us, Jesus showed us what God the Father is like and how we can please him. We know that God instructed us with many symbols intended to bring understanding to men and women everywhere, such as gender distinctions, marriage, sexual relations, beauty, language, sacrificial symbolism, and meaning itself. We also know that God punishes harshly when symbolism is broken. Not only is he patient and merciful but also principled and firm. God gives us the knowledge of good and evil and many biblical stories intended to warn us against doing evil or breaking the symbols God has laid down.

God has given most people a lifetime in which to reach out and find him. Despite the many proofs of God's power, most people of the earth will continue in their rebellion. They will ignore the knowledge available to them and ignore the Holy Spirit who is always at work convicting the consciences of people everywhere of their sin, of God's righteousness, and of the coming judgment.[338] They go about their daily routine of eating, sleeping, making money, having friends and

---

[338] John 16:8–11.

family, and having fun, all without speaking a word of thanks to God. Day after day, year after year, most nonbelievers borrow from God the ability to think, see, hear, and enjoy the world around them. They enjoy fair weather, safety, and many other good things—all without much concern about where these blessings come from or what happens after they die. God is very patient thus far but one day, his patience will run out. God owns the universe and the earth and everything in it. It is the ungodly who ignore the symbolism that God has designed in us and ignore the warnings God has placed in the Bible, describing what will happen to the ungodly on Judgment Day.

Symbolism matters to God now just as much as it has in the past. It is how God thinks, it is how he relates to us, and it is how we relate to God. The symbolism of sex and marriage is probably the most intimate system of symbols that God could have created. It reveals his heart toward us. He breathed his Spirit into every human being demonstrating the tender love he has toward each one. What else could God have designed to show us his love for his creatures other than the new love between bride and groom? That is the love with which he loves us, but in these last days, that all-important symbol has also been demolished and those who still hold to that ideal will soon be persecuted to their deaths, showing the depth of the contempt that mankind has toward their Maker. Can any man imagine marrying a wife who never spoke to him? (Some have jokingly wished for that). Not seeking a relationship with God defies the symbolism built into marriage.

Marriage was once respected as the sweetest of symbols, tasted and respected by billions of men and women of every culture through the ages. It has now been judged by recent generations in the West as detestable—barely worthy of consideration. What, exactly, is left for God to do? He will slowly take back what was stolen from Adam and Eve by Satan, God's greatest enemy. The Lord Jesus—the only one worthy—will peel off the seven seals of God's scroll, symbolic of his ownership of the entire world. Once the destruction of the earth's abusers is complete, the Lord Jesus will return to rule as the victorious King and put an end to all those who oppose him and destroy the beauty of his character through broken symbolism. He will turn symbolism into fulfilled reality, taking those who loved him to the end and making them his very own bride.

The West has reached a point where what matters most to God no longer has any meaning to us. We have become deaf to the symbolism God so desperately wants us to understand. And just like Moses, who did not regard speaking to the rock as having any real importance, we will also suffer consequences if we do not respect the importance of remaining faithful to our spouses and respect the basic meaning and purpose of God creating us male and female.

Symbolism is how God thinks. We must learn to live according to his meaning for the world and not our self-serving, materialistic lusts and desires. What pursuit of mankind is worthier of our attention than a covenant relationship with our Creator, as mirrored in human marriage? Only when we live in harmony with God's symbolism will we have peace with God, love God from a pure heart, and one day be unashamed to stand in his presence. As Christians, we should be much more diligent in teaching these things to the world around us. We must never stop engaging and instructing nonbelievers how much symbolism means to God by living unashamed according to those principles God has established, with the help of the Holy Spirit.

Thanks be to God for the symbolism in Scripture that reveals to us, in some small part, how God thinks.

WORKS CITED

Aland, Barbara et al. *Nestle-Aland Greek New Testament, 27ᵗʰ Edition with McReynolds English Interlinear.* Federal Republic of Germany: United Bible Societies, 1993. eBook. Logos Bible Software 7.19.

Aristotle. *Poetics.* MIT. Trans. S. H. Butcher. 3.XXI–XXII. Web. October 15, 2011. <http://classics.mit.edu/Aristotle/poetics.3.3.html>.

—. *Posterior Analytics.* Trans. G. R. G. Mure. MIT. II.7. Web. March 2, 2019. <http://classics.mit.edu/Aristotle/posterior.2.ii.html>. (Qtd. in Chandler).

Augustine of Hippo. "On Christian Doctrine." I.2.2. *Christian Classics Ethereal Library.* Calvin College. n.d. Web. March 2, 2019. <https://www.ccel.org/ccel/augustine/doctrine.iv.ii.ii.html>.

—. "On the Morals of the Manichæans." *St. Augustin: The Writings against the Manichaeans and against the Donatists.* Ed. Philip Schaff. Trans. Richard Stothert. Vol. 4. XVIII.65. Buffalo, NY: Christian Literature Company, 1887. eBook. A Select Library of the Nicene and Post-Nicene Fathers of the Christian Church, First Series. Logos Bible Software 7.19.

Bauernfeind, Otto. "*Mataios.*" *Theological Dictionary of the New Testament.* Ed. G. Kittel, G. W. Bromiley, and G. Friedrich. Vol. 4, pp. 519–524. Grand Rapids, MI: Eerdmans, 1964. Strong's Greek #3153.

Behe, Michael. *Darwin's Black Box.* New York: Free Press. 1996. Print.

Bennett-Smith, M. "Biblical Marriage Not Defined Simply as One Man, One Woman: Iowa Religious Scholars' Op-Ed." *Huffingtonpost.com.* Updated February 2, 2016. Web. March

4, 2019. <http://www.huffingtonpost.com/ 2013/06/06/bibli-cal-marriage-iowa-scholars-op-ed n 3397304.html>.

Beredjick, Camille. "Biblical Scholars: Actually, 'Traditional Marriage' Isn't Just One Man and One Woman." *Patheos*. June 5, 2013. Web. 4 March 2019. <http://friendlyatheist.patheos.com/2013/06/05/biblical-scholars-actually-traditional-marriage-isnt-just-one-man-and-one-woman/>.

Block, Daniel Isaac. *The Book of Ezekiel, Chapters 25–48*. Grand Rapids: Wm. B. Eerdmans Publishing Co., 1997–. Print. The New International Commentary on the Old Testament.

Boyd, Gregory. *Satan and the Problem of Evil*. Downers Grove, IL: InterVarsity Press, 2001. Print.

Bruce, F. F. *New Testament History*. New York: Doubleday, 1969. Print.

Brucker, Gene A. *Renaissance Florence*. Berkeley: University of California Press, 1983. n.pag. ACLS Humanities. E-book. March 2, 2019.

Caldwell, Jim and Penny Caldwell. "Split Rock Research." *SplitRockResearch.org*. Web. March 3, 2019. <http://splitrock-research.org/content/Welcome/>.

Canterella, Eva. *Bisexuality in the Ancient World*. New Haven, CT: Yale Nota Bene, 2002. Print.

Chafer, L. S. "Angelology." *Bibliotheca Sacra*. 98.392. p.408. (1941). Dallas: Dallas Theological Seminary, 1941. eBook. Logos Bible Software 7.19.

Chandler, Daniel. "Semiotics for Beginners." *Princeton University*. n.d. Web. 5 August 2003. <https://www.cs.princeton.edu/~cha-zelle/courses/BIB/semio2.htm >.

—. *Semiotics, The Basics, second ed.* London: Routledge, 2007. Print.

Cicero. "Roman Law: The Art of the Fair and Good? The Protection of Citizenship." *in Verrem*. 2.5.165. *University of Cambridge School Classics Project*. Trans. C. D. Yonge. Web. March 4, 2019. <https://www.romansinfocus.com/sites/www.romansinfocus.com/ files/Protection%20of%20citizenship.pdf>.

Collins English Dictionary. "Humanism." *HarperCollins Publishers.* Web. March 2, 2019. <https://www.collinsdictionary.com/us/dictionary/english/humanism>.

Conzelmann, Hans. "*Skotizo.*" *Theological Dictionary of the New Testament.* Ed. G. Kittel, G. W. Bromiley, and G. Friedrich. Grand Rapids, MI: Eerdmans, 1964. Strong's Greek #4654. E-book. Logos Bible Software 7.19.

"Cousin Marriage." *Focus on the Family.* Web: March 1, 2019. <https://www.focusonthefamily.com/family-q-and-a/relationships-and-marriage/cousin-marriage>.

Crick, Francis. What Mad Pursuit: A Personal View of Scientific Discovery. New York: Basic Books, 1988. (Qtd. in Meyer's Signature in the Cell). Print.

Dickson, Andrew. "Spy Report That Criticised Marlowe for 'Gay Christ' Claim Is Revealed Online." *The Guardian.* March 30, 2017. Web. March 4, 2019. <https://www.theguardian.com/stage/2017/mar/31/christopher-marlowe-spy-baines-note-gay-christ-british-library-online>.

Dictionary.com. "Metaphor." Web. January 19, 2012. <www.dictionary.com>.

Du Rand, J. A. "Groups in Jewish National Life in the New Testament Period." *The New Testament Milieu.* Ed. A. B. du Toit. Vol. 2. Halfway House: Orion Publishers, 1998. n.pag. E-book. Logos Bible Software 7.19.

Durant, Will. *Caesar and Christ. The Story of Civilization.* Part III. New York: Simon and Shuster, 1944. Print.

Dworkin, Andrea. *Intercourse.* New York: Basic Books, 1987. Web. March 4, 2019. <https://www.feministes-radicales.org/wp-content/uploads/2010/11/Andrea-DWORKIN-Intercourse-1987.pdf>.

Edersheim, A. *The Life and Times of Jesus the Messiah.* Book III, ch.6. New York: Longmans, Green, and Co. 1896. E-book. Logos Bible Software 7.19.

Elwell, W. A., and Comfort, P. W. "Timeline of Biblical Events." *Tyndale Bible Dictionary.* Wheaton, IL: Tyndale House Publishers, 2001. p. 1337. Illustration. E-book. Logos Bible Software 7.19.

Fiensy, D. A. "Crucifixion." *The Lexham Bible Dictionary.* Ed. J. D. Barry et al. Bellingham, WA: Lexham Press, 2015. E-book. Logos Bible Software 7.19.

Foerster, Werner. *"Exestin." Theological Dictionary of the New Testament.* Ed. G. Kittel, G. W. Bromiley, and G. Friedrich. Vol. 2, pp. 560–575). Grand Rapids, MI: Eerdmans, 1964. eBook. Logos Bible Software 7.19. Strong's Greek #1832.

Galloway, Lt. Col. Charles A. Honor Roll: 276th Infantry Regiment. Web. https://www.trailblazersww2.org/pdf/paulvancellettess.pdf. [sic] Retrieved 8/11/2019.

Gilman, Charlotte Perkins. *Women and Economics: A Study of the Economic Relation Between Men and Women as a Factor in Social Evolution.* London: G. P. Putnam's Sons, 1900. p.149. eBook. March 3, 2019. <http://www.gutenberg.org/files/57913/57913-h/57913-h.htm>.

Goldsheider, Ludwig. *Michelangelo: Paintings, Sculpture, Architecture.* London: Phaidon, 1975.

Gomez, P., Gunten, A., and Danuser, B. "Content-Specific Gender differences in Emotion Ratings from Early to Late Adulthood." *Scandinavian Journal of Psychology, 54,* 451–458. 2013.

Gonzales, Guillermo and Richards, Jay W. *Privileged Planet.* Washington, DC: Regnery. 2004. Print.

Gosling, J. C. B. "Hedonism." *The Oxford Guide to Philosophy.* Ed. T. Honderich. New York: Oxford University Press, 2005. Print.

Hamilton, Victor P. *The Book of Genesis, Chapters 18–50.* Grand Rapids: Wm. B. Eerdmans Publishing Co., 1995. Genesis 22:1–19. Print. The New International Commentary on the Old Testament.

Holy Bible: English Standard Version. Wheaton, IL: Crossway Bibles, 2016. Print.

Hughes, Anthony. *Michelangelo.* London: Phaidon Press, 1997. E-book.

Hurley, James B. "Did Paul Require Veils or the Silence of Women? A Consideration of 1 Cor. 11:2–16 and 1 Cor. 14:33b–36." *Westminster Theological Journal* 35.2 (1972): 190–220. eBook. Logos Bible Software 7.19.

Jabr, Ferris. "What Is Beauty For?" *New York Times Magazine*. January 12, 2019. p. 22. Web. February 28, 2019. <https://www.nytimes.com/2019/01/09/magazine/beauty-evolution-animal.html>.

Jesus Christ: The Greatest Life. Ed. Johnston M. Cheney. Trans. Stanley Elissen. Eugene, OR: Paradise, 1999. Print.

Josephus, Flavius. *The Works of Josephus: Complete and Unabridged*. Trans. William Whiston. Peabody: Hendrickson, 1987. n.pag. Logos Bible Software 7.19. E-book. 17.10.272.

Justin Martyr. "Dialogue of Justin with Trypho, a Jew." *The Apostolic Fathers with Justin Martyr and Irenaeus* (vol. 1, ch. 89–90). Eds. A. Roberts, J. Donaldson, and A. C. Coxe. Buffalo, NY: Christian Literature Company, 1885. E-book. Logos Bible Software 7.19.

Lane, William L. *The Gospel of Mark*. Grand Rapids, MI: Wm. B. Eerdmans Publishing Co., 1974. E-book. Logos Bible Software 7.19. The New International Commentary on the New Testament.

Louw, Johannes P., and Eugene Albert Nida. "*Malakos*." *Greek-English Lexicon of the New Testament: Based on Semantic Domains*. New York: United Bible Societies, 1996. eBook. Logos Bible Software 7.19. Ref # 88–281.

McClain Alva J. "The Greatness of the Kingdom: The Mediatorial Kingdom in Old Testament Prophecy." *Bibliotheca Sacra*, *112* (1955). p.107. E-book. Logos Bible Software 7.19.

McNeill, John J. *The Church and the Homosexual*. Kansas City: Sheed Andrews and McMeel, 1976. Print.

Meyer, Stephen. Signature in the Cell: DNA and the Evidence for Intelligent Design. New York: HarperCollins. 2009. Print.

Michelangelo. "David." *Michelangelo, Early Life*. Michelangelo.com. Web. <http://michelangelo.com/buon/bio-index2.html?>. <http://michelangelo.com/buon/bio-early.html>. October 3, 2009. Also qtd. at <http://essayss.net/showthread.php?p=775>. March 2, 2019.

Missler, C., and M. Eastman. *Alien Encounters*. Coeur d'Alene, ID: Koinonia House, 1997. Print.

Myers, A. C. "Jewish Revolts." *The Eerdmans Bible Dictionary*. Grand Rapids: Eerdmans 1987. n.pag. E-book. Logos Bible Software 7.19.

NET Bible. *The NET Bible First Edition*. Biblical Studies Press. 2005. eBook. Logos Bible Software 7.19.

New American Standard Bible: 1995 update. LaHabra, CA: The Lockman Foundation, 1995. E-book. Logos Bible Software 7.19

Origen. "Origen against Celsus." *Fathers of the Third Century: Tertullian, Part Fourth; Minucius Felix; Commodian; Origen, Parts First and Second*. Ed. Alexander Roberts, James Donaldson, and A. Cleveland Coxe. Trans. Frederick Crombie. Vol. 4. Buffalo, NY: Christian Literature Company, 1885. E-book. The Ante-Nicene Fathers. Logos Bible Software 7.19.

Oswalt, J. N. *The Book of Isaiah, Chapters 1–39*. Grand Rapids: Wm. B. Eerdmans, 1986. Isaiah 14:1–4. Print. The New International Commentary on the Old Testament.

Oxford English Dictionary. Compact Edition. "Metaphor." Oxford: Oxford University Press. 1971. Print.

Pascal, Blaise. *"Pensées." Christian Stack Exchange*. VII(425). Web. November 4, 2018. <https://christianity.stackexchange.com/questions/2746/where-does-the-concept-of-a-god-shaped-hole-originate>.

Peirce, Charles. *Collected papers of Charles Sanders Peirce*. Ed. Charles Hartshorne and Paul Weiss. 8 vols. Cambridge, MA: Harvard University Press, 1931. (Qtd. in Chandler). Print.

Pelliccia, Hayden. "Symposium." *Selected Dialogues of Plato*. Trans. Benjamin Jowett. 190. b, c, d. New York: Random House, 2000. Print.

Pickett, Tom. "Population of the Pre-Flood World." N.p. Web. February 21, 2019. <http://www.ldolphin.org/pickett.html>.

Plato. "Cratylus." *Plato in Twelve Volumes*, Vol. 12. Trans. Harold N. Fowler. Cambridge: Harvard University Press; London, William Heinemann Ltd. 1921. Web. 2 March 2019. 384d. <http://www.perseus.tufts.edu/hopper/ text?doc=Perseus%3Atext%3A1999.01.0172%3Atext%3DCrat.%3Asection%3D384d>.

Rhoads, John H. "Josephus Misdated the Census of Quirinius." Ed. Bruce Chilton. *Journal of the Evangelical Theological Society* 54. 2011. n.pag. E-book. Logos Bible Software 7.19.

Rudd, Steve. "The Exodus Route: 22 stops from Mt. Sinai to Kadesh Barnea." *The Interactive Bible*. Web. March 3, 2019. <http://www.bible.ca/archeology/bible-archeology-exodus-route-sinai-kadesh-barnea.htm#thirtyeight>.

Sartre, Jean-Paul. "Being and Nothingness." *Existentialist Philosophy*. Ed. James A. Gould and Willis A. Truitt. Encino: Dickenson, 1973. Print.

Scarbrough, Roy. "When Michelangelo Made an Ass of His Critic." *Hubpages.com*. Web. March 3, 2019. <https://hubpages.com/art/When-Michelangelo-Made-an-Ass-of-his-Critic>.

Scarry, Elaine. *On Beauty and Being Just*. Princeton: Princeton University Press, 1999. Print.

Schmitt, David P. "Are Women More Emotional Than Men?" *Psychology Today*. n.pag. Web. February 28, 2019. <https://www.psychologytoday.com/us/blog/sexual-personalities/201504/are-women-more-emotional-men.>

Schrenk, Gottlob. "Ekdikos." Ed. Gerhard Kittel, Geoffrey W. Bromiley, and Gerhard Friedrich. *Theological Dictionary of the New Testament*. Vol. 2, pp. 442–446. Grand Rapids, MI: Eerdmans, 1964. E-book. Logos Bible Software 7.19. Strong's Greek #1558

Steinberg, Leo. *Michelangelo's Painting: Selected Essays*. Ed. Sheila Schwartz. Chicago: University of Chicago Press, 2019.

Strong, James. "Sakak." *Enhanced Strong's Lexicon 1995*. Woodside Bible Fellowship. E-book. Logos Bible Software 7.19. Strong's Hebrew # 5526.

Swanson, James A. *"Mizbeakh." Dictionary of Biblical Languages with Semantic Domains: Hebrew (Old Testament)*. Oak Harbor, WA: Logos Research Systems, Inc., 1997. eBook. Logos Bible Software 7.19. GK #4640.

Symonds, John Addington. The Life of Michelangelo Buonarroti, Based on Studies in the Archives of the Buonarroti Family at Florence. Vol 1. Third ed. New York: Charles Scribners Sons, 1911.

Turley, Jonathan. "Polygamy Laws Expose Our Own Hypocrisy." *USA Today.* October 3, 2004. Web. March 4, 2019. < http://usatoday30.usatoday.com/news/opinion/colum-nist/2004-10-03-turley_x.htm>.

Unger, Merrill F., "The Old Testament Revelation Concerning Eternity Past." *Bibliotheca Sacra.* 114.454 (April 1957). p.140. E-book. Logos Bible Software 7.19.

Van Der Toorn, Karel., Bob Becking and Pieter W. Van Der Horst. "Melqart." *Dictionary of Deities and Demons in the Bible.* Second ed. Grand Rapids: Wm. B. Eerdmans,1999. Print.

Woods, Sarah McDavitt. "Jesus was a Rape Baby." *Medium.* November 10, 2017. Web. February 28, 2019. https://medium.com/@ artscisarah/jesus-was-a-rape-baby-98e652f2d8f8. 11/10/2017.

Xenophon, "Memorabilia." *Xenophon in Seven Volumes.* Ed. E. C. Marchant. 2.1.21–33. Cambridge, MA: Harvard University Press, 1923. Web. April 18, 2016. <http://www.perseus.tufts.edu/ hopper/text?doc=Perseus%3Atext%3A1999.01.0208%3A-book%3D2%3Achapter%3D1%3Asection%3D33>.

Scripture Index

Subject Index

www.ingramcontent.com/pod-product-compliance
Lightning Source LLC
Chambersburg PA
CBHW021619120626
46545CB00001B/310